With Singleness of Heart

With Singleness of Heart

by

GERALD KENNEDY

". . . with singleness of heart as to Christ himself . . ."
EPHESIANS 6:5 (Moffatt)

HARPER & BROTHERS, PUBLISHERS

NEW YORK

This is for

My Colleagues of the Portland Area

Contents

Preface

Preachers are the most wonderful people in the world. They are critical and kind, serious and humorous, sensitive and brave, humble and proud, tough and gentle, dramatic and sincere. I would rather be with them than with any other group. To be accepted into their fellowship and receive their friendship is a blessing greater than any man deserves. No earthly honor can ever give me greater satisfaction than to take my place in this wonderful fraternity of preachers.

When the late President J. N. R. Score invited me to deliver the Slover Lectures at Southwestern University in 1950, I accepted with particular pleasure because they were to be on the general theme of the ministry and directed to preachers. His death in 1949 was a great loss to the ministry and a great sadness to me personally. But I know he must rejoice with all of us in the Church at the wise choice of his successor. President William C. Finch is an outstanding educational leader and he made my week in Georgetown most enjoyable with his many kindnesses.

These lectures are not expected to make any profound contribution in the academic field. Their observations and conclusions rise out of one man's attempt to analyze few achievements and many failures, and to learn from the ministries of great colleagues. If they help any man enter into a deeper appreciation of his high calling, I shall be glad.

GERALD KENNEDY

Portland, Oregon

With Singleness of Heart

1

The Double-minded

... but this one thing I do ... Philippians 3:13

THE business of living is complicated enough in the best of times, but its chief difficulty is a failure to observe certain fundamental and simple rules. Our entanglements and our frustrations are not because we are confused by complicated directions which we are not wise enough to learn. They are due to our careless disregard of plain principles which a wayfaring man, though a fool, can comprehend. A great deal of good counseling is nothing more than bringing back into consciousness a moral law taught us since the first grade. But we forget. We try to reach our destination without remembering what we learned about the terrain.

When we took up golf (and what a crucial moment that was) we were told a few very simple rules. Perhaps the most important one was: Keep your eye on the ball! Of course! Even a man who never played the game in his life can comprehend that. Its obviousness is tiresome. Yet most of the bad shots in all the days that follow are due to forgetting or ignoring that simple rule. We can hardly believe we are so stupid as to take our eyes away before the ball has been hit. Not until a companion assures us that, before the club head has made contact with the ball we

13

are looking up to see what happened, will we believe we are guilty. For some of us golf is a constant effort to go back to this simple, obvious rule. It is a matter of getting into trouble and extricating ourselves (temporarily) by remembering and practicing an elementary precept. So it is with life!

The simple rule for adequate living which is basic and yet universally ignored is: Be single-minded. This is to life what "keep your eye on the ball" is to golf. It does not need to be argued for people to believe it. Hardly anyone will question its wisdom, and its very obviousness is what makes it trite. But the myriad of alluring things which beckon make us forget to keep a single purpose in our mind. We forget to ask if this new goal is a part of the purpose we have accepted for ourselves. Or is it, perhaps, a denial of the real purpose? Can the two things be harmonized? Does the attainment of one automatically prevent the attainment of the other? Is our present way of life a breaking of the simple command to be single-minded?

There is no man more in danger of cracking up on the rock of double-mindedness than the artist. In this category I include the preacher, for preaching that is worth anything is art. Every preacher can learn much from the great artists, for the disciplines are similar. And so are the temptations! The man who is especially gifted will be under greater temptation to dissipate his energies than the man who has only one talent and knows it. This may be the reason the single-talented man so often has much more to show for his life, comparatively, than the ten-talented man.

The very nature of the task of the ministry is a temptation to double-mindedness. Ours is a wide and varied responsibility. Everything is grist for the preaching mill. Our service is as wide as life. The demands upon us are limitless, and they would strain the powers of a genius. In an age when other professional men are encouraged to specialize, the ministry still demands the all-round man. In striving to be all things to all men, we can easily succumb to the temptation to become self-contradictory creatures. When that happens, one part of us cancels out the other part, the end result being a kind of chameleon creature, with neither integrity nor effectiveness.

John Dos Passos has a word for us:

No durable piece of work, either addressed to the pulps or to the ages, has ever been accomplished by a double-minded man. To attain the invention of any sound thing, no matter how trivial, demands the integrated efforts of somebody's whole heart and whole intelligence. The agonized efforts of split personalities to assert themselves in writing have resulted, on the money side, in limp pandering to every conceivable low popular taste and prejudice, and, on the angels' side, in a sterile connoisseur viewpoint that has made "good" writing, like vintage wines and old colonial chairs, a coefficient of the literate rich.[1]

Willa Cather stressed the same significant point in a letter to the literary critic Maxwell Geismar:

Listen, my friend, no man can give himself heart and soul to one thing while in the back of his mind he cherishes a desire, a secret hope for something very different.

The man who suffers from this condition may never end up in an asylum. He may never feel the need to be psychoanalyzed or be forced to take treatments from a psychiatrist. He probably will wonder with increasing bitterness why he fails to achieve anything permanently satisfying and why other men, perhaps lesser men, accomplish those achievements. He may go faster and faster in a desperate attempt to salvage something out of his career. He may watch a puppy or a kitten chase its tail with the horrible suspicion that there is the best symbol of his own running in circles. He may wonder why he cannot have the peace and

[1] Wilson, *The Crack-Up, A note on Scott Fitzgerald,* New Directions, 1945.

quietness in his own heart which he preaches about and urges other people to attain. Yet with all of his wisdom which he has accumulated from a wide reading, he has never learned the simple admonition of Jesus:

The light of the body is the eye: if therefore thine eye be single, thy whole body shall be full of light. (Matthew 6:22)

It is probably true that there are times when it is easier to maintain the single mind than others. Perhaps we live in a particularly difficult time for single-mindedness. When men do not have faith in tomorrow, it is difficult to determine what they ought to be doing today. An age of doubt and materialism provides a field day for the double-minded complexes. But on the other side of the picture, times like these have a greater need for men to demonstrate how to live at peace in the midst of confusion. If the Christian faith can create spirits which know unity in the midst of chaos, it is a sure sign of its eternal validity. This is a great day for the preacher precisely because it is a day terribly in need of his witness. Instead of complaining about the difficulties, let us thank God that He has given us a task which commands our whole heart, our complete mind, and our entire strength. But before our healing work can be done, we must ourselves be healed.

It is rash to hold up one characteristic and say that it is the secret of our Lord's greatness. But I cannot escape the belief that one of the main threads which runs through his perfection is an astonishing singleness of mind. One has the feeling that he never tried to combine incompatibles. We insist that he was a man and made choices, and we do right in that insistence. But there is something quite different in his choices and ours. We decide whether to follow God's way or our own; whether to serve God or Mammon; whether to do what we know is right or what we know is wrong. There is nothing of that reflected in the choices of Jesus. His decisions concerned which of two ways was closest to his Father's will. His ultimate commitment had been made and he never wavered from it. We do! There is in him, because of this, a simplicity and a perfection which never was seen before or since on sea or land. It is the attainment of this state which John Wesley called *Christian Perfection* and for which he insisted every man ought to strive. In our own best moments, we know we cannot escape the inner compulsion to seek it until we find it.

I. Disease

It is not easy to understand one's own time. Experts do not even agree on the essential nature of past generations, and when men are in the midst of a period, it is even more difficult to separate the essential from the merely apparent. Most of us have become wary of taking too seriously the contemporary diagnoses which come from the press with startling regularity. Perhaps the age between the two world wars is best designated *The Aspirin Age*. Perhaps we are in the midst of the *Decline of the West*. Quite possibly this is our *Time of Troubles* and we are in the closing years of a *Sensate Culture*. But as Christians, we believe that the present crisis is the inevitable result of trying to live without God, or worse than that, of trying to manipulate God for our own use.

As a result of this, men have lost sight of the central value. When the main purpose of man is no longer to love and serve God, he finds himself attracted irresistibly by many side issues. For materialism by its very nature cannot provide the singleness of purpose which is religion's achievement. An inevitable concomitant of doubt is double-mindedness. Our generation is disappointed and shocked by the divisiveness of the world, and reluctantly it has given up its dream of *one world*. But our failure was inevitable, for there can be no unity among the nations or among people without a unity of belief that every man owes something to his neighbor because he owes something to God.

Let us get over this nonsense that the world can be united through trade, or fear, or humanism. The disease continues its progress because hardly anyone recognizes its basic cause and its cure. The foundation of a society is its belief in an ultimate loyalty, and when there is no such belief, there is no sure foundation. That which makes us persons is a conscious recognition that all we are worth is what we are worth to God. When God goes, our health goes and we are torn by cross-purposes which destroy us.

Now it would be nice if we could believe that the ministry was miraculously free from this disease. It is not! God builds no walls around His servants to keep them safe from the slings felt by ordinary men. The minister's life is particularly vulnerable to this disease. It is not without significance that the professional religious leader has been so often in the past the chief stumbling block in the way of God's purpose. If there is any man particularly tempted to forget the single purpose of his life, it is the preacher. In some ways, our Catholic brothers are in a safer position. They at least wear a special garb and sacrifice the experience of family life. But Protestant ministers often lean over backwards to minimize any distinctions between them and their laymen. Whether we like it or not, this is the way we have chosen, and we believe, all things being considered, it is the best way. But let us not be unmindful of the added difficulty in keeping clear the conditions of our service.

The popular preacher, especially, can easily forget the single loyalty demanded by his profession. There are times when he mistakes the voice of the chairman of his board for the voice of God. It is easy to think the community's clamor is the speech of righteousness. There may be times when the demands of his denominational machinery ought not to be heeded. Every man will go wrong not once but often, unless he keeps clear the single duty of being a good minister of Jesus Christ. Once anything else is given equal recognition, he will succumb to the disease of double-mindedness.

The minister may desire prominence in other fields, if his talents are up to it. He may be a clever after-dinner speaker and much in demand. This will give him a wider hearing, he tells himself, and it will certainly increase his earnings, which he does not emphasize consciously. He may become active in other organizations and put more time in them than he does in his Sunday school, for example. He may spend a great deal of time in lecturing on how to bring up children or in reviewing books. He might conceivably spend too much time writing books. The point is only that once a man puts personal popularity and success alongside his duty to his Lord, the single purpose of his ministry disintegrates, and great is its fall. A contemporary theologian spoke a true word to us all when he said:

Caricatured by the Devil, the absurd is on the contrary the fixation of a temporal reality in the infinite or in the unquestionable: the idea of success in itself, or power or riches in themselves. There lies Hell.[2]

When this disease progresses very far, it becomes a scandal to the ministry. I believe more harm is done by double-minded preachers than by all the sinners in the world. Many a man has had his faith shattered when he came to the sad conclusion that his minister was a pious fraud. For if the man who proclaims God's word to the people on Sunday reveals during the week that this is only his way of getting what he wants for himself, he is much worse than the man who follows that path without vain pretense. Any man who searches his own heart knows that he is infected with this disease of the world. Only by being aware of it and praying constantly for an extra portion of God's grace can he keep his soul in health and his mind single.

The sermon becomes a vague dullness or an interesting

2 de Rougemont, *The Devil's Share,* Pantheon, 1944, 109.

nothingness if the preacher is double-minded. It may have no life because the preacher has lost the sense of his divine calling. It may entertain but not redeem if the preacher is seeking to please the congregation first and God second. Our safety is to preach with one aim and one desire—to speak the word God wants spoken and be the channel through which God can probe the hearts of the congregation. This is so simple that it solves all the preacher's problems and answers all his questions. It brings peace and assurance.

When it comes to pastoral work, double-mindedness plays havoc. What are we trying to do? Serve people or build an organization? Massage the egotism of men who have had far too much of that treatment already? Report a large number of calls? Get added names on our roll? The truth is that none of our activities shows less result for the energy expended than pastoral calling ungoverned by any single purpose. The same is true of our community service. We can spend more time serving on more committees and accomplishing less, than in almost any other activity I know. Many a preacher thinks he is a community leader when he is only a community errand boy. The Church is concerned with the community, but not from the standpoint of the chamber of commerce or the real estate board. It is concerned from the viewpoint of Christ. Let the preacher never forget whom he represents and let him ever be mindful of the kind of community person Jesus was. If we had his mind, there are some community projects we would be too busy to bother with, and there are some neglected areas we would enter at once.

The New Yorker has a sharp, satirical view of the modern scene and often it has a cartoon which every preacher ought to see. Some time ago the magazine had a Whitney Darrow drawing which showed two ministers conversing in a comfortable, luxurious library. Said the older man to the younger: "Drawing upon my not inconsiderable experience, Andrews, my advice to a young man ambitious of preferment in our calling is to steer

clear of two subjects—politics and religion." I have known
preachers who followed that advice. They sometimes referred to
vague labels which would offend no one because no one knew
what they meant. They talked a saccharine kind of nonsense
which passes in this decadent time for religion, but sickens any
man who has read his Bible. If a man loses sight of the single
valid reason he is in the ministry, he may end up like this. God
forbid!

II. CAUSE

Jesus was not alone in being led to a high mountain and shown
the kingdoms of the world. We cannot read the temptation story
with only academic interest. Every man stands where Jesus stood,
but in a particular way the minister enters into that temptation
experience. For he, too, must make fundamental decisions regarding the methods and goals of his work. Shall he depend on
the promise of bread, or a miracle, or compulsion? One of the
significant chapters in every minister's autobiography is the one
dealing with the time he must stand on the mountaintop and
decide, as Jesus did. Unfortunately, this is the chapter which is
nearly always omitted.

We tend to lose our eternal perspective. The world is too much
with us. Like our contemporaries, we regard men as creatures to
be used. Of course we want to use them for good purposes and
we encourage them to do something for the Church. But we
forget that the will of God is that each man should be converted,
completely, while we heal too many men lightly. Finally we are
content to obtain from as many as possible a little service for our
organization and, incidentally, increase our own personal reputa-
tions. We are content to become trouble shooters or emergency
repair men. We no longer see our task as announcing God's
absolutes. We are servants of the relative, hoping to patch up a
few broken dreams and comfort a few mangled spirits. At last
we are content to keep the machinery running and interpret the

ruthless selfishness of our society with a few well-chosen pious platitudes. We blow up the inconsequential and play down the serious sins. As it was said of Goldsmith, we make goldfish talk like whales. But we make leviathan lisp sweet nothings.

There is a finality in Jesus which, when recognized, saves a man from the confusions of multiple purpose. It is hardly too much to say that, unless our Lord is a finality, he is nothing. But there are many men who would take him casually, and one of the bad results of Biblical criticism has been the false assumption that Jesus' finality has been destroyed. Experience has driven many of us back from this quicksand to the firm foundation of Paul's insistence that "God was in Christ." The preacher who has no clear experience of Jesus' lordship will have no certainty of his authority.

A contemporary philosopher has given us an interesting definition of "decadence." He says it means "the dropping of the object." [3] The artist, for example, who substitutes mere self-expression for loyalty to an objective principle of landscape painting, has become decadent. The man who has come to believe that moral ideals are nothing but personal feeling has "dropped the object," for he has thrown overboard the saving, necessary principle of life. In the field of Christianity, decadence sets in when we have dropped the authority of Jesus Christ. After that disaster, we are the victims of a hundred alluring goals, the end of which is personal disaster. For men have to accept some ultimate command, or they find themselves vainly trying to obey everybody's command. They usually end up by becoming the slaves of the most raucous voice of the competing demagogues.

The half-committed preacher is of all men the most miserable. I think the minister's life is either the most satisfying of all, or else it is the most unhappy. If we cannot believe that our commission comes from God, we are poor creatures trying to put dignity into a calling which has become nothing but a dignified

[3] Joad, *Decadence*, Philosophical Library, 1949.

hypocrisy. One of the difficulties of our task is the necessity of steering the narrow sea between the rocks of a Messiah complex and a commissionless calling. To change the figure—the anchor which holds us steady in the midst of storms and contrary winds is the knowledge that, for better or for worse, we are Christ's men, with his seal upon us, called to be his servants and his spokesmen.

This lack of authority produces double-mindedness, which, in turn, makes us speakers about Jesus instead of his spokesmen. One of the sure signs we have lost our singleness of life is to preach as if we had to flatter God instead of speak His word. George A. Gordon and his brother went to church in Old South Church, Boston, one Sunday. When they came out, he asked his brother what he thought of the sermon. "It was a good sermon for Paul," the brother replied, "and I am sorry he was not there to hear it." [4] Preaching is not saying nice things about Jesus or Paul. It is being captured by the spirit of God revealed in their lives, and speaking to this day as they would have us speak. The disease which weakens our preaching power is caused by our decadent tendency to drop the object, which is the authority of Jesus Christ.

III. Cure

Max Eastman spoke words about a speech which might well be spoken of a preacher's life:

A speech has only one dimension; it starts at the beginning and flows to the end. You cannot spread it out, or carry it back and forth, or take it here and there. You cannot dig around under it. A speech should be rapid, clear and energetic, and make but one main point. It should run like a river between high banks, the floods of emotion adding to its force, but never widening the territory it covers. This cannot be accomplished extemporaneously except once or twice in a

[4] Quoted by Phillips, *Bearing Witness to the Truth*, Abingdon-Cokesbury, 1949, 130.

lifetime; it cannot be accomplished by taking successive starts from a series of penciled notes. The more impassioned the language the more it will in these circumstances tend to expatiate and meander. All great orators have known this, and all great orators, from Deuteronomy and Demosthenes to Daniel Webster and Mark Twain, have written their speeches and learned them by heart whenever they could. A great orator is both a dramatist and an actor; he can write as though he were speaking and he can speak as though he had not written; he can act the part of himself.[5]

There is in this paragraph a good description of what our lives ought to be. We need that same directness and the sense of inevitable movement toward a single goal. With the passing years we may come to live that way without taking thought. The part we must play somewhat self-consciously at times, becomes our natural self if we do not deviate. Increasingly as the years go by, we become the servants of one master and the spokesmen of one message. This is not to say that our lives must become narrow and confined. Quite the opposite! But all our varied interests and activities become the interesting variations of a single and powerful theme.

The most restless, distressed preachers I know are the ones with their eyes on the main chance. They are all reaching and never attaining. They are all criticism and no peacefulness. Their journey seems to be a constant worry about where to change trains and which train to take from the next station. They are so anxious not to be forgotten that their very obsequiousness makes them invisible. What a relief it would be for such men to believe that whatever God wants them to do He will find a way for them to do it. One of the reasons Paul is such an inspiration to me is that he shows how an ambitious man can find peace in a complete committal to Christ. If God can cure a man like Paul, He can cure a man like me. If a tempestuous genius like the Apostle could be healed of double-mindedness, ordinary persons like most

[5] Eastman, *Enjoyment of Living,* Harper, 1946, 313.

of us can certainly find our healing. In this surrender to God, we have the guide to so many vexing problems. When William Penn asked George·Fox whether a Quaker should wear a sword, Fox replied, "Wear it as long ·as thou canst, William." So when we wonder if we should do this or that, we may rest in the assurance that we will know if our minds are single.

One of the themes which runs through much of the writing of Dostoevski is an insistence that there is little hope for a generation of double-minded men. The cure begins when they have been captured by a single authority. It is not in escape from duty that freedom lies, but in commitment. The fear of our day is a spiritual fear which assails men caught in the trap of their multiple aims. Serenity is the gift of wholeness, and wholeness comes to men who have given their lives to the one "whose service is perfect freedom." The final test as to whether we have been cured of our divisiveness is whether or not we live without nervous tension. The minister's health cannot stand the strain of the terrible demands upon him unless he has learned to leave the ultimates in the hands of the God whose servant he is.

Someone said to Dr. Campbell Morgan one time, "You can preach and you know it." To this Dr. Morgan replied: "I have no hesitation in affirming I *can* preach. I do not know anything else under the sun of which I am willing to make a similar affirmation. I am sure I dare not say I can sing, and no friend of mine would suspect me of saying I can play golf. I can preach. It is the one thing I want to do and cannot help doing. I would do it as a recreation if I was not permitted to do it as a vocation." [6] Not all of us could announce with the same assurance that we can preach, yet we should be able to say with the same certainty that the ministry is the thing we have to do, and if it were not our livelihood, it would still be our chief joy. For if the ministry is no more than a means of making a living, we are sick. But if it is not only our living but our life, then we have been

[6] Gammie, *Preachers I Have Heard*, Pickering, 1945, 197.

cured of the double-minded disease which takes such great toll among our brethren.

IV. HEALTH

There is a kind of divine simplicity and nobility about single-minded ministers of Christ which makes us envious and ashamed. Take, for example, Cardinal Mercier's will. This servant of God who lived his life in such simplicity wrote:

I have not much to leave. I am possessed of no private means and the little I have earned by the exercise of my functions and by my publications, I have always endeavored to use in good works, living only from day to day. The few small savings which may be found at my death should be employed in meeting any arrears of my household and the expenses of my funeral, and everything over, used for charitable purposes and educational institutions.

There is in this a judgment on our hectic, pagan lives, and we wish we could know this spirit in our own living.

Or take the example of John Wesley. Because he was himself the early Methodist organization, rumors grew up as to his supposed wealth. When England was raising funds for the war with the American colonies, Wesley was commanded to make due entry of his silver plate that it might be taxed. His answer is famous:

Sir, I have two silver teaspoons here in London and two at Bristol. This is all which I have at present; and I shall not buy any more while so many round me want bread.[7]

His finances were controlled by his devotion. However else we may interpret Wesley's experience of the heart "strangely warmed," we cannot escape the conclusion that it was the creation of the single mind.

[7] Quoted by Luccock and Hutchinson, *The Story of Methodism*, Abingdon-Cokesbury, 1949, 193.

There is in our contemporary life an almost pathological desire for peace of soul. But in all our seeking we try to achieve it by some surface trick or manipulation. We assume that there are little exercises which will stimulate the outer level of our minds and perform the miracle. A vast number of people who flock to the Christian heresies of our day go in the vain hope that peace of mind is something to be attained without profound spiritual alterations. It often works for a while, and if the person is not too honestly realistic, he may fool himself for a long time.

But the religious experience of peace is so all-inclusive and profound that it transforms all a man's life, including his motives and his sense of values. It creates a new environment and sets up new dimensions. It creates new definitions of success, happiness and comfort. It is so devastating in its transformation that the New Testament speaks of it as a new birth, a new man, a new kingdom. I was in the South some time ago, holding a series of revival meetings. One night the song director announced an old and familiar hymn, "O Happy Day." But that night I noticed a phrase at the beginning of the third stanza which never stood out before. It seemed to sum up the religious experience perfectly when it said: "Now rest my long divided heart." The healing of the Great Physician is the unifying of our warring divisions and placing them under the control of the single mind.

We can be in the ministry a long time and still be in need of this healing experience. There is nothing automatic in the process by which the professional servant of Christ receives peace in his heart. Like another disciple, he can follow "afar off." The restlessness and unhappiness of many a preacher is simply a sign that his heart is still divided. But when by God's grace we allow Him to work the miracle of healing in us, we shall know a serenity which puts us beyond the reach of fear and self.

Besides knowing peace, the single mind knows power. A novel speaks of a missionary in these words:

Said Lanark, "Bonifay looks so well-fed and cozy, but he's a courageous man. He'll get up early for the purpose of going out and risking death among the Western tribes. He is also a man of education. Unlike Fathers Galtier and Ravoux, in St. Paul, he has read books—though not as many as he would like you to think. And he is more dangerously single-minded than even the fanatical Mr. Harge. I'm never sure that Bonifay won't convert me some day." [8]

Even a writer who is not famous for his spiritual perceptions was wise enough to see that there is power in the single-minded.

The danger which any man with merely vague inclinations toward decency faces when he is against the narrow fanatic, is his lack of power. There is terrible might in the man who has just one ultimate loyalty. He divides and conquers his opponents. That is why single-minded men with inadequate theologies convert more people than the cultured brethren who do not know just what they believe. Yet we do not need to be narrow-minded fanatics to know the power which these extremists often demonstrate. We need only to yield our lives completely to our Lord and make his will our final loyalty. Power is not in the narrowness but in the fanatical devotion.

One of our modern mystics has said something helpful in understanding this whole matter:

For until we love God perfectly His world is full of contradictions. The things He has created attract us to Him and yet keep us away from Him. They draw us on and they stop us dead. We find Him in them to some extent and then we don't find Him in them at all.[9]

The clue, of course, is to "love God perfectly," and then we know that life makes sense and we can assume our place in God's unity.

Singleness of mind will take us through many a difficult place

[8] Lewis, *The God-Seeker*, Random House, 1949, 175.
[9] Merton, *Seeds of Contemplation*, New Directions, 1949, 22.

and help us conquer many a subtle temptation. Remember John Bunyan's reply to his jailor when, after twelve years in jail, he was promised freedom if he would agree to quit preaching.

"I am determined," Bunyan replied, "Almighty God being my help and shield, yet to suffer, if frail life may continue so long, even till the moss shall grow over my eyebrows, rather than to violate my faith and make a continual butchery of my conscience." [10]

The ministry always has need of that spirit, but the day seems to be approaching when our very survival depends on it. In such a time as this, may we find our place among that heroic company of God's good servants, the single-minded.

[10] Quoted by Martin, *To Fulfill This Ministry*, Abingdon-Cokesbury, 1949, 16.

2

The Critic

You only have I known of all the families of the earth: therefore I will punish you for all your iniquities. Amos 3:2

THE critic's place in society is always an uneasy one. He has no secure position, for by the very nature of his task, his is seldom a popular or comforting word. If he pleases one, he is almost sure to displease the other. About the best he may hope for is toleration, and far more often he must expect active opposition and hatred. He will be ridiculed by the artist because he himself is not an artist and yet he professes to judge art. He will be attacked by the public who seem bent on letting themselves be exploited, and so often, with a curious human perversity, turn on those who would be their saviors and champions. He will know the pressure of special interests who are willing to reward the man with a blunted sense of integrity. The critical function is not the one most conducive to peace and ease.

The critic has no abiding city. He is from the first until the last a citizen of a kingdom unseen by human eyes—the kingdom of perfect sincerity and honesty where every man gives the best he has, not for reward, but for the sake of the work. He is driven by a hunger for the best. He can never get used to shoddy work or dishonest administration. He is the sworn enemy of all betrayers of their trust and their talent. He has nothing but scorn for the man who prostitutes his abilities, and he tracks down the fakes and the betrayers with the persistence and ruthlessness of a hunter.

But the critic always acts on the assumption that his attack is directed against men who know better. He does not waste his steel on the poor fellow who has no ability and is so stupid he cannot see his own lack of talent. He speaks to the man who knows the best and who can create the best, if he will. He is a judgment on those who have betrayed their own best selves and their own best work. In all other instances, he simply tells as gently and directly as possible that the artist must content himself with his own level and not strive vainly to create something far beyond him. If a man persists in striving for the creation of something not within the scope of his talents, then the critic must loose his big guns on him. But his word is primarily for those who know but do not practice. As Amos said it, God punishes most severely those whom He knows, and the prophet, like the critic, speaks to guilty spirits.

The critic, therefore, must be a man of faith. He must believe in men and their possibilities. He must believe that God has given each man a sense of responsibility and that no man denies that sense without feeling guilty. He believes in ultimate standards which no amount of clever, modern manipulating can change or distort. He believes that he has a duty to Someone beyond himself, and loyalty to that One is more to be desired than personal popularity or profit. In other words, the critic, whether he realizes it or not, is a religious man and takes his stand on the side of the angels.

If we should use the literary critic as an example, we might say that criticism cannot be divorced from character. Any man who commits himself in regard to any piece of work is reflecting what he is in himself. He is telling the world what he likes and what he appreciates. Criticism is intensely personal, and art cannot be judged by mechanical regulations. There is always the indefinable, the indescribable qualities which are felt by the sensitive spirit but which cannot be described adequately by simply learning rigid rules. In this field there is no help but in the quality of the critic's life. If he is the right kind of man, he will sense when something is not quite right, even when he could not say precisely what is wrong with it. He will also be able to appreciate the extra goodness in a work, where the insensitive spirit will pass it by. If the critic is not necessarily the skilled artist, he is always the skilled appreciator. And he is always the skilled detector of the essentially second-rate, even when it has been covered up with elaborate effort.

The personal nature of criticism is particularly noticeable in our newspaper columnists. They pretend to be objective commentators on the news of the day, but they are always more than that. They have their standards, or lack of them, their likes and their dislikes. They reveal the kind of men they are in every column they write and readers learn to make allowances for their special interests. When, for example, Westbrook Pegler reveals his prejudicial point of view day after day, no sensible man will regard his judgments as objective. Such a one has become a propagandist and, I suppose, has his reward. But he is no longer a trustworthy critic. The most important and necessary characteristic of a good critic is that he should be a good man. He must be honorable. He must be willing to subordinate himself to his task. He must be more than a dilettante. He must have a deep respect for men and a real sense of obligation to serve them honestly.

Now we should never forget that the Christian Gospel is a word of judgment on the world. The Fourth Gospel has this clear understanding of Jesus' work when it speaks of light as a judgment on the darkness.

And Jesus said, For judgment I am come into this world, that they which see not may see; and that they which see might be made blind. (John 9:39)

The Gospel has this double nature in that it helps blind men to see, but it also reveals that some men have preferred darkness to light. Jesus was a critic who illuminated the darkness, but he revealed also the unconscious darkness in which so many men dwell.

When it is at its best, Christianity is never the champion of the *status quo*. In 1879 the first organized strike took place in Sweden. The strikers wanted to have morning prayers and invited a clergyman to conduct them. His reply was to call the police who in turn called out the military to force the strikers to return to their work.[1] No one should suggest that a Christian minister must always be on the side of the strikers. But neither is he automatically against them. He is on the side of justice and he must always take his stand with those who are fighting for justice. His criticism is not to be bound by class or race.

Only the man who has yielded himself completely to the service of God can be trusted as a Christian critic. There is no part of our work which demands more singleness of mind than our prophetic or critical function. Here is where so many men become class voices and apologists for a special point of view. We can easily become dogmatic pleaders for special interests. We are to be critics with our hearts immersed in the will of God as revealed by Christ, and never men who have equated that Will with some particular economic or social movement. I cannot help but add, however, that the Christian prophet will find himself more often on the side of the underprivileged and the disinherited than on the side of the comfortable and successful.

I. NECESSITY OF CRITICISM

John Ruskin in *Unto This Last* speaks of "five great intellectual professions, relating to daily necessities of life. . . ."

> The Soldier's profession is to defend it.
> The Pastor's is to teach it.

[1] *Man's Disorder and God's Design*, Harper, II, 1949, 78.

The Physician's is to keep it in health.
The Lawyer's is to enforce justice in it.
The Merchant's is to provide for it.

He goes on to say that "on due occasion" each man must be willing to die for his profession.

The Soldier, rather than leave his post in battle.
The Physician, rather than leave his post in plague.
The Pastor, rather than teach falsehood.
The Lawyer, rather than countenance injustice.
The Merchant—what is his "due occasion of death"?

The part of this we are interested in here is the insistence that the pastor may come to the place where he must choose death rather than teach falsehood. The minister, Ruskin is saying, has an ultimate obligation to truth and the maintenance of truth. Here is a clear definition of the critical function and its importance. There may be times when a man is tempted to dodge the issue or move too cautiously, but when he is speaking for God, he must speak the truth or die. For a society cannot long endure if it has no men whose sworn duty it is to tell the truth about its own life as well as the life of its enemies. Let us come to terms with this at the very beginning of our work, and let us know that compromise here is death to our souls and dishonor to our profession.

No people can long endure without an ultimate standard. Something has to be accepted as an absolute, the betrayal of which is a tragic sin. For when men deny that there is an objective reality to which they must be loyal, there is no repentance possible because there is no sense of guilt to bring them any sense of their need to be forgiven. Even the most primitive tribe is wise enough to teach its children that there is a final loyalty. A nation which has wandered too long in the wasteland of conflicting standards finally turns in sheer desperation to worship at the shrine of nationalism. Nothing in all the maelstrom of modern sophistication has been so utterly stupid as the idea that men can live with no keystone loyalty.

Relativism has been our fetish and it has well nigh been our destruction. Today we are beginning to reap the results of this madness, and in a day when we need something to keep us steady, we are caught in the whirlwind of partial devotions. We need to believe and reform. We need the sense of ultimate principles to which we can give ourselves with faith that they will keep us steady and establish our wavering destiny. But we have been so infected with the relativistic virus, that we take refuge in screaming loudly against our enemies and taking refuge in mere armaments. We have accepted the double standard with a vengeance. It is wrong if you do it, but right if I do it. It is wrong today but it will be right tomorrow. It was wrong under those circumstances, but it is right under these circumstances. We have not had enough strong voices warning us against this madness. The deterioration of any art begins when it substitutes personal feeling for objective reality. The downfall of a people begins when it assumes that it can play fast and loose with moral laws and each man can do what is right in his own eyes. For this threatening debacle we ministers are not guiltless. Perhaps we could not have stemmed the tide under any circumstances. But certainly we have too often become a part of the disease instead of performing the healing function of the Christian critic.

The moral processes are in constant need of interpretation. The critic is such an interpreter, and he has to be able to say which way God is going to move. He must have some word about the long plans of the Almighty. He will not be able to perform this part of his task because he is wiser than other men or more gifted, but he will be able to do this necessary thing if he does not forget that God's ways of dealing with men do not change. His is the task of showing a generation when it is departing from the principles of the good society as they have been announced

in the Bible. His ways do not change with the changing generations. When a man is himself amenable to God's will and listens
faithfully to His voice, he earns the right to say, "Thus saith the
Lord!"

The literary critic is not merely a censor, but he is obligated to
maintain the standards of good taste. So does the Christian critic
hold up the standards of spiritual life. When one reads the novels
of our time, he is aware of how much pressure there is being
exerted constantly to degrade the taste of the people. There are
those books which are obvious attempts to gain a wide reading
by pandering to the fascination which smut has for too many
readers. But there are others which in some ways are worse,
because they degrade the taste without being quite so obvious.
They hide under a horrible cover of imitation decency, though
their interpretation of life is insincere and vile. Writing, like
living, is always in danger of being overwhelmed by the spirit
which justifies anything if it pays. One wonders what would
happen to a nation's literature if every critic were silenced and
no man were permitted to shout, "This is trash, and its creator
ought to be hanged."

There is a profit in degrading the taste of the people in any
field. One of the discouraging things about our society is to note
the number of people engaged in the high enterprise of trying to
minister to the worst in men. Pressure is exerted to open up the
regulations against indecency. When we consider the wealth
which is earned from this legalized vice, we wonder if it is possible to stem the tide or even keep it from completely overwhelming us. Of one thing we may be certain, and that is the necessity
of building some kind of dyke against this flood. For the only
safety finally is in clear voices describing tawdriness and filth for
what it is and in building up the taste and courage of people who
will not allow the degradation to have its way.

People so seldom seem to realize what is happening to them
until it is too late. How easy it is to be touched by the slow stain

of the world without any sense of the disaster taking place. The hunger for purity can be dulled. In the name of being practical, we are urged to legalize gambling and raise money for charity by lotteries. Because it can never be completely eliminated, the so-called realists urge the legalizing and controlling of prostitution. In less spectacular matters, the pressure is always on us to give a little here and retreat a short way there. But once these siren voices are heeded, it is only a question of time until a people is debauched and a generation is betrayed. Against this tendency there is the need for clear-thinking critics who will warn against the ultimate outcome of such policies and stoutly maintain the moral standards.

How easily the public can be influenced! Apparently if you have enough money to pay for enough advertising, you can make a vast number of people believe anything. Hitler knew this and used his knowledge to create his monstrous system. Selling experts know it and the public is often gullible enough to buy large promises and small values. We go from one extreme to another. Mark Twain once commented that if a cat sits on a hot stove lid it will never sit on another, and that is good. But it will never sit on a cold one either. It overlearns its lesson, and so do we. The people need clear-eyed, morally sensitive critics to protect them against their exploiters and against themselves.

When John Wesley returned from Herrnhut to London, he found most of the pulpits closed to him because of his brother Charles' reputation for enthusiasm. The name Wesley was anathema to most of the London rectors. The difficulty was that Charles had been preaching as if what he said mattered and would affect every man's life who listened and believed. This would upset the comfortable parishes and disturb the peace. For Wesley's preaching was a judgment, not so much on the poor sinner, as on the comfortable saint. Yet it was the word which that time needed to hear, and it was the saving word for eighteenth century England. The critic need not expect to be received always with open arms, but he should know that the world has great need of him and God's servant can neglect this part of his work only at the peril of his soul.

II. CHARACTER OF THE CRITIC

The critic must be a man of faith and the Christian critic will undertake his work with the conviction that, if he has the mind of Christ, he is the speaker for God. The modern definition of faith which seems to me the closest to the Christian concept, was formulated by Kirsopp Lake. Said he, "Faith is not belief in spite of evidence; it is life in scorn of consequence." [2] Underlying this definition there is the whole matter of what we have called "single-mindedness." There is a kind of divine recklessness about Christian faith which is just the opposite of the stodgy, safe attitude so often equated with religious living. The man of faith has gone all out for something. He has risked everything on "one turn of pitch and toss." He has come to the place where he is willing to trust completely his Lord's commands. It is no longer a matter of edging ahead fearfully and cautiously, but marching forward without a backward look or a single regret. Beyond everything else, the preacher in his role of critic has to live his life "in scorn of consequence."

The man of faith is always a brave man and we ought not to minimize Christ's demand for courage. As a listener once said to John Wesley after hearing him preach on the demands of the Christian life, it takes more courage than Alexander the Great's. The Son of God goes forth to war, and we are those who have promised to follow in his train. But it is a courage which always manifests itself in love and service. There is nothing of the egocentric exhibitionism characteristic of so much of what the world calls courage. Strangely enough, the man who best practices it seems least conscious of it. It is a secondary product coming out

[2] Quoted by Luccock, *In the Minister's Workshop*, Abingdon-Cokesbury, 1949, 179.

of the Christian's complete devotion and final loyalty to the truth of God in Christ.

Cornelia Otis Skinner, in her personal recollections,[3] tells about her father as a young actor going to Europe with an American dramatic company. They took with them their own critic, paid his salary while he lived and traveled with the company. Yet he was supposed to write objective criticisms of their productions for the press. She says that no one seemed to think there was anything questionable or inconsistent in the arrangement. Most of us would suspect the reliability of such a man's judgment, even if we believed completely in his intelligence and his good intentions. It is not humanly possible to write objectively when a man is under obligations to the ones he writes about. Even Alexander Woollcott was no exception to this general principle. He was one of the top names in the field of dramatic criticism and he was intimately acquainted with many of the leading figures of the stage. But while his writing was alive and interesting, his criticism was not always reliable, and friendship sometimes dulled the edge of his judgment.

We may move into another kindred field and look at literary criticism. If you have ever been called on to review a friend's book, you know what a serious problem it may present. If it is a good book and you can be enthusiastic about it honestly, the problem disappears. But if the book is not very good, in your judgment, you must either be honest and perhaps lose a friend, or keep the friend and be dishonest with the readers. Many a man, I suspect, tries to steer a middle ground, which satisfies nobody. There was one reviewer who stated his attitude in these simple words: "A reviewer who will not give a friend's book a good review is a louse." That is clear enough, but the man with some conscience toward his profession will not find that advice too helpful.

All of this suggests that the critic must maintain a certain

---

[3] Skinner, *Family Circle,* Houghton Mifflin, 1948.

objectivity if he is to keep the edge of his criticism sharp. It is a dangerous thing for a preacher to get hopelessly under obligation to some man or some group of men in his church. Our temptation is to move too much with those who can make contributions to the church and to us. We become so entangled in our personal relations that we simply cannot bring ourselves to say a critical word about these good fellows. Then we become the spokesman for a group or a class. I wonder if it is a good thing for a man to accept a new car or a house from one man in his congregation. This is probably sour grapes because no one ever offered me either of those things. But I have known men whose messages seemed to me definitely conditioned by their unconscious obligations. At least we might all agree that the critic who speaks for Christ must sometimes speak a word to his friends, which they will not like to hear. Other things being equal, the freer he is, the more likely will his courage rise equal to the situation.

The critic must be a man with a sense of discrimination. He may not be able to create the best. Perhaps he cannot preach the greatest sermon or do the best job of administration. He may not be able to step into the social or political scene and play the lead. His writing may never win the award. But he must know the best when he sees it and love it. For this, he must keep close to God, for only the man who has learned to look at life and men through the eyes of Jesus Christ can be trusted to speak the right word. The fact that we have been ordained into the Christian ministry does not guarantee that our opinions will always be right. Let us learn a lesson from St. Paul. We must discriminate between the times we say things of ourselves and the times when we have a direct mandate from God. Only the disciplined life and the tender conscience will wait for a divine assurance before speaking. Courage without discrimination will work havoc in the church and bring shame to the whole prophetic function of the ministry.

It was the great gift of Jesus never to let ideals take his attention from men. In Jean-Paul Sartre's play *Red Gloves,* the Leader says to a young revolutionary, "You do not love men; you love only your ideals." There is a kind of priestly pride which can blind a man to his fellow men, and it is a terrible thing. Whenever we come to prefer announcing a policy over healing a man, we are wrong. Which is to say, the critic must be governed by love and his hatred of the cheap rises from his knowledge of what it does to the souls of men. Too little has been made of the prophet's temptation to pride. There is a kind of man who prides himself on speaking frankly at all times, who needlessly hurts people and is nothing but a boor and a sadist. Perhaps the little girl had this in mind when she prayed, "O Lord, make all the bad people good, and all the good people nice." If we must speak the word of judgment, it will be a good thing if, like Jeremiah, we weep as we speak.

The critic has to be a man of experience. He has to have a wide knowledge of art and life. He should be a true cosmopolitan and feel at home in all places. He will not be shocked and flutter about in a horrified manner, because he has looked at the worst. The preacher who can be shocked might as well lock his counseling room, because it will never be used for serious work. He needs the power to listen to any story and look into any black depth of degradation and not retreat. No man will learn more about the depths to which human beings can descend than the Christian minister. But if he looks at life steadily, he will be aware also of the adequateness of Christ's healing power. He will often be profoundly saddened, but he will never be shocked.

The Christian critic's experience will help him see through the false claims and the hollow bravado of so much modern living. His job is to help people see what they really want in life. He must tear aside the tinsel and show the tawdriness underneath. His is the thankless task of showing how much of what we spend our time in pursuing we do not want. As Father Stanton of St. Albans remarked, "If God gave us all we asked for, I should think we should most of us be in hell by this time." [4] We are to be interpreters of human life, human desires, and human destiny.

III. CRITICISM AS PRESSURE

In this day of high pressure salesmanship, it may not be pleasing to define criticism as pressure. But there is a gentle urging which God exerts on men and nations, and His representatives must press constantly in the right direction. We are not thinking of an external, ruthless pressure exerted to get what we want over the rights of others. We are thinking of the pressure our conscience puts upon us and the discontent which comes from a vision of the best.

There is a terrible period of waiting that comes to the man who has just published a book. It is the time when he waits for the reviews. Perhaps the genius is saved from this suspense, but the ordinary man wonders if, after all, he should have exposed himself so completely to the eyes of the public. He feels a sense of shame that there is written down for men to read the inner workings of his mind and the witness of his spiritual quality. Did he have anything to say? Should he have worked it all over once more? Was it wise to include that last chapter? In an agony of suspense he waits for the critics to pronounce their judgments.

More particularly, he waits for a particular man to speak his mind. There is one who, above all the others, he trusts. If the rest should speak well and this one man should speak ill, his book would be a failure. And so the poor author waits for the word like a prisoner at the bar waiting for the jury's verdict. Through one man there may come the pressure to create the best he can. He might satisfy the average reader, but it is no good unless the one critic sees in the work evidences of honest effort and significant achievement.

This, in a sense, is the position a minister ought to hold in his community. If he is worthy and has been with them long enough,

[4] MacLean, *High Country*, Allenson, 1934, 59.

he may expect to stand among his people with a critic's mantle on his shoulders. The underworld may eye him apprehensively. The selfish interests, who would exploit the community if they could, will regard him fearfully. Out of past experience they know how keen his eye is in discerning their devious ways. The city council will ask itself, "What will he say about this ordinance, if we decide to pass it?" The whole city may be conscious of a continuous pressure upon it, gently but persistently urging it toward righteousness. Community leaders will find themselves asking, "What would he think, and worse, what would he say, about this deal I am contemplating?"

This is the position a church ought to fill in a democratic society. We Protestants believe in the separation of Church and State. We will fight any group or any church which tries to break down this separation. We believe in the public school system. But we do not believe that the Church is to have no dealings with the State. We do not believe that there is a realm where the Church is to be excluded and an area where its voice is not to be heard. We believe that a Church in a democracy is to be the conscience of the nation and bring every national policy into the light of the Christian judgment. What the critic is to art, the Church ought to be to society. There is a sense, therefore, in which the Church is to be a pressure group, but it is not to be seeking favors from the government or from the taxpayers which will benefit itself as an institution. It is to push toward virtue and away from vice, and it is to be an organization always on the side of goodness. It is to be severe in its attack on tyranny and immoral politics. It is not to drift with the tide, but it is to be a vital force with which every administration and every group will have to reckon.

The Christian critic creates shame. One of the astounding things about men is their ability to feel shame. This is the reason for the secrecy which surrounds all nefarious practices, for if men know what is going on, they will not stand for continuous ex-

ploitation of the young and the weak. There are many things
men will not do if they are sure they will be observed. Secrecy is
the enemy of decency and hardly any man wants to stand before
his fellows as one who is profiting from human degradation.
Shame is the ally of goodness and many a man is shamed into
better living.

I embarrassed a man very much one time, quite innocently.
There was a case of discrimination in one of our institutions and
I announced loudly and confidently that there was one man on
the board who would never stand for it if he knew about it.
He took up the cudgel with me in a rather hesitant, curiously
chastened manner, but he stood shoulder to shoulder with me.
I learned afterward that he had known about it all the time and
had not dared speak against it. Sometimes God uses us in co-
operation with a sense of shame, to get His work done.

On August 3, 1914, King Albert of Belgium was given an
ultimatum by the Germans. He was urged to give the German
Army free passage and thus escape the destruction of his land.
The alternative was a forced passage with the outcome hardly
in doubt. But King Albert never hesitated and the passage was
refused. In speaking about it afterward he said that Belgium had
been "cornered into heroism." Sometimes God expects us to
corner men into goodness.

IV. Criticism and Conservation

There is something about the Church which rises above the
crosscurrents of any particular time. Imperfect as it obviously is,
it has enough of the eternal truth within it so that the passing
centuries do not leave it behind. An English writer has said this:

The only place in our world today where a Christian citizen of the
Roman Empire of the second or third century would feel at home
would be the Church. In every other institution he would be completely at a loss. Democracy—Capitalism—Socialism—Fascism? These

would mean nothing to him. But in a church service, his heart would kindle. "I believe in God the Father Almighty, Maker of Heaven and Earth, and in Jesus Christ, His only Son, our Lord, who was conceived by the Holy Ghost, born of the Virgin Mary, suffered under Pontius Pilate, was crucified, dead and buried. He descended into Hell. The third day He rose again . . . I believe in the Holy Ghost, the Holy Catholic Church . . . " The very same words he used to recite in Rome or Antioch or Alexandria or Athens or Corinth so long, long ago.[5]

The minister makes a great mistake when he associates himself automatically with a group just because it is radical. This is the path to spectacular failure. The radical idea may be no more than a passing fad and the radical preacher may be only a faddist, for the radical thing may not be the true thing and there is no certainty that just because a thing is new it is right. If we look back over the last few years we shall see what a variety of new movements within the Church were going to save it. They made a small contribution, but they did not work any profound reforms. The men who led them have had to come back into the fold somewhat shamefacedly confessing that they had mistaken a half-truth for the whole truth. There is an insatiable hunger in some men for the new as an end in itself. They do not succeed in building the Church, but they are experts at tearing down the old. They may experience a certain destructive exhilaration, but they are not the real servants of the Church.

On the other hand, there are those who are inevitably associated with every reactionary movement within and without the Church. It is never a matter of what is right and what is wrong, but rather, what is established and what threatens change. They would have been on the side of the Pharisees in the first century, and they have made every effort to transform Jesus into a historical mummy in the twentieth century. They are usually

[5] Davies, *Secular Illusion or Christian Realism,* Macmillan, 1949, 84.

about one generation behind, though in some matters their lag is even greater.

In between these two extremes there are the men who strive to be citizens of the Kingdom of God. May we be saved from being either radicals or conservatives! We are members of a Kingdom which knows nothing about time but is founded on the eternal realities of God. Its laws do not change and its foundations are never shattered. This is our home and we are commissioned to judge the contemporary scene in the light of its principles.

There are times when the Christian critic will seem radical because he will challenge an established custom in the name of the Kingdom where God's justice rules. There are times when he will seem conservative because he will question the throwing aside of some essential principle without which we can have no strong and secure life. But always, his aim is to conserve, not tear down. It is easy to be brilliant when one is being merely negative. The sermon which defines what is wrong can sparkle, but the sermon that has some positive aim is not so easy to prepare. We are not called to be critics in order to tear down, but to build up; for the evil of the cheap and tawdry is that it gets in the way of the noble and the best. When our word must be a destructive one, it is simply to clear the site so that men can build their lives in harmony with the real Kingdom.

Admiral Emory S. Land once gave Harry Hopkins the title of "Generalissimo of the Needle Brigade." [6] The Christian minister also has to be adept at needling. But we must make sure that our motives are right and we must never lose sight of our ultimate goal. We shall go wrong unless our minds are set on building and conserving and our hearts are full of love. Which is to say that at no time is the single mind more essential than when we are being critical.

[6] Sherwood, *Roosevelt and Hopkins,* Harper, 1948, 282.

3

The Pastor

And he gave some . . . pastors and teachers . . ." EPHESIANS 4:11

WE SHOULD never lose the significance of the fact that the majority of people refer to us as pastors of the Church. I have heard men speak with the deepest affection of their "pastor." We have many other functions to perform in our ministry, but this one seems to reach deepest into the hearts of our people. The 23rd Psalm is on the lips of more people more times because it brings us great comfort to think of God as our shepherd—our pastor. Yet there is no part of our work that can be so relatively ineffectual, because it is so diversified. A consistent, continual ministry in this field is not more common because many a man never succeeds in focusing his eye on the main purpose of the pastor.

G. K. Chesterton said that a lunatic is not a man who has lost his reason but a man who has lost everything except his reason. That is a strange saying, but it is a profound one. When men sacrifice everything for the intellectual pursuit, they become unbalanced and less than whole. There is a kind of madness which possesses them and infects all their activities. The man who surrenders his spiritual and emotional life for a career of pure reason has chosen the path to madness.

47

It may be that this has been the wrong turning taken by our modern civilization. The optimism which was characteristic of the West fifty years ago was based on a false assumption that we had passed beyond the necessity of faith. In the old days of the race's immaturity, this viewpoint intimated, it was all right to believe what you could not prove, but in the latter days, science had spoken to us and now we should base our lives on intellect alone. The time was visioned when every action and every motive could be scrutinized, analyzed and made the subject of a syllogism. So enamored have we been with this false hope that we attempted to make human life a mechanical affair and the legitimate object for study on the part of faithless experts. It would be a good thing to remember Chesterton's warning: in this direction lies lunacy.

This has not worked, though it is curious to note how difficult it is for men brought up in this tradition to surrender it. They will not go back to church and they will not sit down with a godly pastor to talk about their frustrations and their fears, but they will pay fifty dollars to consult a psychiatrist. They are suspicious of priests, but they still believe in their secular counterparts. There seems to be something about paying a fee and going to the office of the psychologist which is scientific and intellectually sound. But to many a modern a call at the office of the local minister still means to be childish and unsophisticated. A man in a Western city makes a living by just listening to people talk about their problems and their troubles; he makes no pretense to be wise enough to heal sick souls. He just listens and people are so desperate to discuss their problems and confess their sins, that they crowd his appointment schedule. Others write to Dorothy Dix.

The meaning of all this seems to be that men are so constituted as to need pastoral help. The idea of a self-sufficient, coldly intellectual creature who lives off the top of his mind, is a myth. The pushing back of the darkness of the unknown is never complete. We cannot escape the mystery of human existence. We can never feel quite at home in the world and security is not to be attained by taking thought. If we push the comfort of religion aside, we find ourselves consulting the fortune tellers, the astrologers and the columnists. The assumptions of atheistic humanism have been broken reeds, and we ought to know at last that God is He without whom we cannot live.

Let Christian ministers, therefore, never doubt the importance of their pastoral work. We have tended to despise this part of our responsibility because we have not truly understood it. We have made "calls" without much thought as to their ultimate purpose. We have gone out for leisurely afternoons of small talk and surface conversation. We have been satisfied to be regarded as well-meaning, friendly men with enough tact to leave at the proper time. We have been fearful of creating a spiritual crisis because it might not seem to be good taste. We have given the impression of being celestial salesmen. And all the time we have despised ourselves secretly for our fumbling, our fearfulness, and our ineffectiveness. We have never dared to face the implications of our Lord's demand to be pastors of his flock.

We will be wrong if we fail to take advantage of all the psychological training possible. It is a good thing that our seminaries are recognizing this part of our work as worthy of a full-time professor. We can learn many truths about the human personality and we can escape many wrong approaches, if we sit at the feet of experts in counseling. At the very least, we ought to read the literature in the field. Yet none of this will be of much benefit to us unless we have the pastor's heart and the shepherd's spirit. Nor will it profit us very much if we cannot learn from our experience and become more skilled in diagnosing spiritual and moral sickness. This is one part of our work where the absence of the loving heart will be noted first, and it is no good to learn the techniques as an end in themselves. The man who was the greatest pastor I ever knew never had an hour of study in the field of counseling, and the man who would be the last one I should ever go to for help was a Ph.D in psychology. We shall not be so foolish as to say that training is not important, but we shall insist that there is no field where training alone can be less effective, than in our pastoral work.

A word of warning needs to be given those who would make psychology their only emphasis in the ministry. There is a kind of disease which attacks some men when they go all out for counseling. They seem to lose their perspective. Every action has to be subjected to their professional analysis and then explained in a professional jargon which has no more reality in it for the patient than Old English has for a high school student. It seems to me that if we assume there is no such thing as a healthy, normal action, we ourselves are in need of treatment. As a matter of fact, there are some leaders in this field who seem to be more in need of treatment than their patients. A man can develop a curiosity about the inner workings of the human mind until he becomes morbid. We had better be on our guard against becoming pious Kinsey investigators. In our pastoral work it is important to see life steadily and see it whole, as Matthew Arnold put it in characterizing Sophocles.

In this day of tremendous churches and intricate organizations, we can hardly escape the necessity of having men who specialize in the pastoral ministry. This is no new thing, however, for Paul speaks of "having then gifts differing according to the grace that is given to us. . . ." Yet each minister ought never to divorce himself from the pastorate. The preacher needs to know and love the people as much as the people need to hear him. The administrator will never do his job effectively if he does not see himself as a servant of the Church and a pastor to the people. For in the Church the cold, intellectual man has no place. As George MacLeod of Iona, Scotland, said:

It is not that our clergy are too intellectual. . . . It is that we are apt to be only intellectual. As an honest old Scotch minister once protested: "The Meenistry of the Kirk O' Scotland is the most eddicated meenistry in the worrld and it has verra nearly ruined the Kirk O' Scotland." [1]

Nearly every preacher with more than average ability has been told many times what a success he would have been in some other profession. He might have made a fortune as a lawyer, or he could have excelled as an insurance executive. Perhaps! But any man who is worth his salt knows that no other profession could have kept him so close to human need. In this, he has had a reward far beyond salary or prestige. For as the years go by, it is being a pastor to the people that brings the lasting joys, and it is here that the test of any man's worth is apparent. Jesus summed up the Last Judgment in terms of the pastoral function with a parable written especially for preachers. We may be brilliant, intellectual and prominent, but if we do not feed the hungry, visit the prisoners, clothe the naked, it is not enough. Let us not despise what our Lord put first.

I. Intimacy of Our Task

There has grown up in our time an idea that the ministry is a sheltered existence, kept apart from life in the raw. We are regarded so often as men in ivory towers, dwelling beyond temptations and aloof from the common plagues of living.

In the early years of my ministry a friend invited me to attend a wrestling match in a neighboring city. He convinced me it was a necessary part of my education, and since the affair was being held some distance away, I went. We sat in a smoky arena surrounded by people who had not bothered to bring their culture along, if they possessed any. We watched one of the most stupid spectacles which even a five-year-old child would not confuse with an athletic event. It was slow, it was dull, it was stupid. I have wondered ever since why anyone ever went more

[1] Quoted by Phillips, *op. cit.,* 157.

than once. On the way home, my friend said to me, "Well, how did it seem to see some real life for a change?" Real life! I remembered the young mother who had come to me the previous week to talk about the future which looked so dismal. Her husband had died leaving her with no income and two small children to support. I thought of the young man whose girl had broken the engagement within a month of the marriage, and the terrible sadness of youth. I recalled the man who seemed to me one of the most self-sufficient men in the community who came to confess that he was in the power of an evil habit he could not break. And this friend of mine thought we had been seeing real life! The average pastor sees more real life in a day than the average man sees in a year. If there is one man who does not live in secluded safety, it is the minister.

We are taken into the most solemn moments of human experience because of our office. When two young people decide to undertake the great human adventure of creating a home, we are the ones who discuss it with them. We stand before them at the altar and speak the beautiful, realistic words of the ritual. It is to us as representatives of God that they make their promises. We are the ones who give them the blessing of the Church. Forever more we are associated in their experience with one of the high moments of their lives and we have a relationship with that family which no other man can ever have.

When a young couple want to dedicate their baby to God, again it is the Christian pastor to whom they turn. No man has such intimate relationships with childhood. From that first meeting at the altar for baptism until childhood is over and mature life is begun, the pastor is given the opportunity to minister in the most profound experiences of youth. Then if he is blessed with a long pastorate, he may baptize the child of one who received the holy rite as an infant from his hand. The families of the church belong in a special way to the pastor. They not only allow him entrance but they welcome him into their homes at all times. In the profound moments, the door is open always to him.

Then when death comes, it is the pastor who is called into the home. He is the present help in time of trouble. He surrounds the broken family circle with the assurance of eternal life and God's love. He stands by the grave to speak the mighty promises of our faith. He creates a healing silence. He is the one to whom the people come in the days of their sorrow, and many a family comes to wonder what they would have done if it had not been for their beloved pastor. In this there is a reward which is above price, and for all the added burdens he must bear, the pastor knows that he is more than repaid. If it seems almost more than he can endure to share the burdens of his people, yet they hold him up with their affection and their gratefulness. One of the many embarrassments of the ministry is the huge dividends of appreciation a man receives for such a small investment of pastoral care.

Because most men's work deals with only partial human relations, they see men incompletely. Their vision is often distorted and blurred. The politician can hardly escape from seeing people primarily in terms of votes. True, they are voters, but the most important part of a man is not in the fact that from time to time he casts his ballot. Nor is it the fact he can be influenced to vote in a certain way. We have had much talk about economic man and no one could deny that this is a significant part of every person. We use goods and we have material needs. We are necessary cogs in the economic machine and there are men who must spend the bulk of their time in thinking of humanity in economic terms. The merchant has to provide for the real or fancied needs of his customers and they are to him potential profits. We shall not be so foolish as to disregard these various aspects of a man, but we must insist that they are not the whole man. Perhaps the reason we mistake what other nations want is that we have too many men in places of power who cannot see man as a whole.

But as pastors we can, and indeed we must, see men completely. We see men as voters, consumers, customers. But we see man in his spiritual hunger and in his personal relationships. We see him under the pressure of terrific tests, and we see him as he relaxes with his friends. This has to be said reverently and carefully, but the pastor comes closest to seeing men as God sees them. They are essentially spiritual creatures with spiritual drives, but no one deals with them in the spiritual realm so constantly as does the minister. He is given every advantage to know men truly.

It is a noteworthy thing that the good pastor gets neither cynical nor disillusioned about men. The academic philosophers may yield to bitterness, but that is because they are out of the struggle itself. They pose as observers who analyze human behavior from the outside. But the pastor can never stay outside. He has to enter into the turmoils and the disappointments; he shares the failures and the betrayals. He enters into the moral failure which has brought ruin to a man's life and home, and he sees the worst and he is aware of the terrific toll of sin. But he also sees the best, and he comes face to face with quiet courage and unassuming nobility. He learns of burdens being carried too heavy for any man to bear. He becomes aware of sacrifices being made cheerfully day after weary day, with no trumpets blowing and no credit given. There are in every congregation enough inspirational stories to fill a book. So often the great things about people are as deeply hidden as their failures, for courage and cowardice alike are qualities not easily discerned. But the good pastor learns to be a spiritual detective, and as the years go by he learns to see what most men are never privileged to behold.

When Arthur Conan Doyle was a young doctor, he accepted an appointment without much enthusiasm because it was the only opening available. After he had been there for some time, a larger opportunity was given him and he decided to take it. But when he was getting ready to leave, he was astounded at the number of patients and friends who, with deep affection, came to tell him good-by. One old woman brought him a valuable plate her sailor son had brought her from abroad. It was all she had, she told him, but she wanted him to have it. He could not keep the tears out of his eyes.[2] How often is this repeated in the life of the pastor! We get ready to leave a parish and the friends come to tell us how much our little efforts have meant to them. Things long forgotten by us have been remembered by them. Words which fell without too much thought from our lips brought healing to stricken lives. We have been given credit for much more than we deserved. Surely, God has reserved His choicest gifts for His pastors.

II. Our Pastoral Opportunity

One of the successful pastors of an earlier generation was Dr. John Mathews. He wrote in his autobiography, "For more than forty years I have studied the easy passes into the human heart." [3] It is a great phrase for the minister to ponder. If the human heart has its hardness and its stubbornness, it has also its easy entrances.

One February I found myself on the east side of the Cascade Mountains in Washington. I needed to go to Seattle for a speaking appointment and the time was running out. After consulting with the highway patrol, I learned that the most direct pass had been blocked with snow and it was questionable whether or not it had been opened. The sure way to get through was to drive north and take a lower road through the mountains, which I did. You may say that this is simply obvious common sense and nothing to write about. Yet is it not true that we deny that same common sense when we are looking for a pass into a man's heart?

[2] Carr, *The Life of Sir Arthur Conan Doyle*, Harper, 1949, 62.
[3] Quoted by Martin, *op. cit.*, 76.

We do not take the long way and we do not wait to learn what the conditions are. We drive directly and with very little finesse at the main object. We do not inquire about or seek the easy pass.

As I look back over my ministry, I am convinced that most of the pastoral mistakes (and there have been many) were caused by lack of patience. Here is a man in trouble which he may or may not understand. But you feel sure that you understand it and so you want to cure him right now. Without any waiting or investigation, you try to force your way into his life. He resents it and with all the good intentions in the world you find yourself locked outside. The pass is blocked. The most serious thing about the failure is that it may raise a barrier which will take years to penetrate, and sometimes the damage is irreparable. If a minister is not willing to take time with a person, he ought not to try a sudden cure. Sometimes it may work, but for every success there will be many failures.

Only stupid people are impressed by high pressure salesmen. I doubt that the methods which are taught in some of the schools are as effective as they are assumed to be. Those little tricks are not hard to see through. The psychological twists which are supposed to force quick decisions are not very subtle. And if there is anything a self-respecting man resents, it is another man's attempt to manipulate him or influence him for an ulterior purpose. This is to treat him as a means to an end and it is utterly destructive of human dignity. Much of our failure is a vain attempt to play the part of religious salesmen instead of the role of pastors.

Trouble is one of the easy passes into the human heart. Whatever mood a man gets in when things are going well, he becomes more teachable when he is in trouble. Suffering and adversity are sometimes the only elements which can open the blocked passes. Hearts hard and impervious to the presence of God are made tender and aware when pride has been brought low. The good pastor is ever alert to the signs proclaiming someone is in trouble.

We shall not always succeed even then, but more times than not a great pastoral opportunity is being given us by another's distress.

I read in the paper one morning that a girl had been arrested on suspicion of murdering her newborn baby. At least the baby had been found in a garbage can and she had confessed it was hers, though she insisted it was dead at birth. As to that, there were no witnesses. Something said to me that here was one who needed a friend and I called at the jail. Gradually, from a stunned, sullen silence, she was able to talk about her life and its tragedy in the days that followed. Partly on my responsibility the murder charge was dismissed. A day came when I was invited to perform the marriage ceremony for her to the young man who was the father of the child. They began their new life on a religious foundation. It does not turn out this way always. Probably we shall have many more failures than successes. But when we have been wise enough to bring Christ's healing grace into even one stubborn heart, we can endure our failures with patience.

Now and again a man faces despair because everything he has counted on has been destroyed. He may stand poised at the deep end of things, wavering for a little while before he makes his final decision. The right word makes all the difference in the world just then. That is why I always have a feeling of guilt when there is a suicide in my community. Someone, even I, should have sensed that terrible despair and gone to the man's aid. We are not wise enough to sense always the crises in the lives of our brethren, but the years ought to bring us greater skill of diagnosis. Jesus could feel the light touch of a woman's fingers on his garment when she was seeking his help. But this is the power given only to men who have the single purpose of service.

The frustrated life is open to the ministry of the pastor. This is a widespread condition in our time, and the task is primarily one of making the inner need conscious. Strangely enough, there are no people more insecure than the successful ones. They are the ones who hide their spiritual poverty behind possessions, but like Zacchaeus, once they see a life that is right, they know their own lack. The largest single group coming to see me as a pastor in the past few years has been the wives of successful men. They have everything they thought they wanted. Cars, clothes, maids, leisure, clubs—all these are theirs. But you do get tired of surface glitter and empty minds after a while. You cannot play bridge twenty-four hours a day. The movies are not possible every night in the week, except for morons. How shall one get through the hours of the day? One can hardly miss this easy pass into their hearts. Let us not be self-conscious in the presence of successful people, because they may have a greater need for our ministry than the poor. We may do our work with the assurance that every man needs the Gospel, and sooner or later every man will provide an opportunity to bring the Gospel to him.

I saw a brilliant preacher fail to win a family for Christ and the Church, and I saw a very ordinary preacher win that family by being with them in an hour of serious sickness. Our preaching ought to be a part of our pastoral work and our sermons should encourage people to believe that, in the Gospel, there is an answer to their dilemma. There is a sense in which the test of good preaching is the number of people who come to see the minister in his study. We cannot answer all the individual problems of the people in the congregation, but we ought to make every man feel that there is an answer to his problem in Christ.

Some years ago a Frenchman wrote a very pessimistic book entitled *A Rebours*. One man finished reading it with this remark, that when a man was in the author's frame of mind, there was nothing left for him but the point of a revolver or the foot of the Cross. Life is constantly bringing us to those situations and we make our choice. We do not always commit actual suicide, but we say no to part of life and kill parts of ourselves. The alternative is the Cross and its redemption. To lead men to the alternative is our pastoral opportunity.

III. STATUS OF OUR PRIESTHOOD

We do not talk very much about the priesthood in our Protestant tradition. Most of our hostages have been given to preaching and the prophetic ministry. This I would not change even if it could be changed. The making of a ritual act the center of the worship service has no appeal to me and the Protestant church should rightly rise and fall with its preaching. But a part of our ministry is best understood if we regard ourselves as priests as well as prophets. We stand in a special position both to God and to the laity. We cannot believe that we are a superior order, but we must accept our responsibility as interpreters of God's ways to men, and interpreters of men's needs to men. If we believe we have the one radical cure for sin, then we are priests, whether we wear a special uniform or not. The argument that seems most valid to me for wearing clericals is that if we are forced to remember more diligently our priesthood, that is good.

We are at the end of the era of "the regular fellow" in the ministry. We have suffered under the delusion that if no one could see anything different in us he would be attracted to the Church. It has seemed to us that by watering down our language we could persuade men to believe in the validity of Christianity. We have assumed that if enough people called us by our first names we were good ministers of Jesus Christ. In contrast to the dignity of older men, young men sometimes go all out for informality because it wins them a certain popularity. When carried to its furthest extremes, ministers have tried to be "one of the boys," by telling off-color stories and playing down their profession as if they were ashamed of it. We have assumed that this was modern and new. It is as old as the Middle Ages and was one of the causes of the Reformation. It was one of the reasons for the Methodist Revival in the eighteenth century.

When the ministry is out on the level of the market place, it loses its power and it must be reformed.

The "regular fellow" has his reward, no doubt, but it is a cheap one. He will be invited to some places which will flatter his vanity. He will be greeted by many people when he walks on the street. He will belong to more clubs than is good for him or his work. He will be asked to deliver numberless speeches largely because he says very little and is brief. But with the passing years there will come bitter disappointments. He will hear of his own members going to other ministers when they need help, and he will watch people go by his door when they are bent on serious errands. He will never know the trust and the deep affection which his less spectacular but more earnest brothers receive. In fact, he knows when it is too late that all of the rewards he has received might have been obtained if he had been a service club organizer or a chamber of commerce greeter. But the spiritual experiences of the pastor have never been his and never will be his.

The problem of intimate friends in the congregation is one each man must solve in his own way. My experience may not be universal, but it has led me to seek my intimate friends either among the ministers or outside my parish. One time when serving a small church in a rather isolated community, I found myself intimately related with a small group in the church. It never seemed just right to me for the sake of my best usefulness. A pastoral relationship can be damaged by too great an intimacy with a special group in the church. There are probably many exceptions to this general proposition, yet let us be aware of the problem and move cautiously in dealing with it. There is a dignity and objectiveness about the pastoral office which has to be maintained. If this is destroyed, the loss is very serious to the people and to the minister.

All of this may sound like a glorification of the "stuffed shirt." This is furthest from my purpose, for if there is one thing to despise and avoid, it is stuffiness. Yet I must confess that I prefer the man who is unconsciously stuffy to the man who consciously is not stuffy. The essential quality is unself-consciousness, which comes to those who are so engrossed in the wonder of their high calling that they play no insincere part. The "regular fellow" can be as obnoxious and unreal as his most stilted, pious brother. The main thing is to strive toward filling the high office of priest in a worthy manner. We shall do it differently, no doubt, and that is good, but we should never make it cheap and trivial.

Because we are priests, we are always on duty. No man ought to go into the ministry if he cannot give himself to it every waking hour of every day in the year. It is more than a profession—it is a life. There is always a child among us taking notes. There is ever virtue or evil going out from us. We are not to be men of contempt and dour indignation, but men of compassion and gaiety. Perhaps we can do no better than keep the master's rules of the sea before us:

To keep cool, calm and collected at all times.
To think first of all lives under my care or command.
To think secondly of all property under my care and command.
And lastly to think of myself.[4]

IV. Pastoral Qualities

The most neglected, and in some ways the most important of the qualities of the good pastor, is an ability to listen. This sounds like a foolish thing to most men because it seems like a purely negative quality. Anyone, they seem to imply, can listen; tell me something difficult to do. My brother, it is not so easy to listen as you think and you do less of it than you realize. Preachers are usually in front of people and usually they are speaking to them. Even when they are not giving a formal address, they are leading

[4] Dod Orsborne, *Master of the Girl Pat,* edited by Joe McCarthy. Copyright, 1949, by Dod Orsborne and Joe McCarthy, reprinted by permission of Doubleday & Co., Inc., p. 39.

the conversation and keeping the talk from lagging. It is easy to get into the habit of speaking constantly, and most of us talk too much.

A fine layman once spoke to me about his minister. He said the man had fine qualities and was doing a very constructive job. "But," he added, "is there any way to persuade him to listen when people call on him for pastoral service? He will not let a person tell his story before he is interrupting and jumping to conclusions." That man's pastoral work is almost nil because people will not put up with that kind of treatment. An important part of the healing process is getting things said which have been frightening because they were amorphous. The too talkative pastor prevents his people from clearing the way for Christ's healing touch.

One Sunday afternoon after preaching in a college town I was visited by a group of students. The minister of the church came in uninvited and interrupted every conversation with a little homily, not always to the point. The students had some things to say, but they never had a chance to say them. Finally we broke up the meeting and I heard that minister say to the students, "Come around any time. I'm always glad to help you." But that man had made it doubly sure that no students would ever bother him again. He could not listen. When a rebel told a Christian friend that if he met Jesus Christ on the road he would spit on him, the reply came quietly, "It would not be the first time." I hate to think what some ministers would have tried to say under those circumstances.

We need sympathy for others. This is one of the easiest things for us to lose, for the minister can become the most egocentric of persons. As a seminary student I was given the assignment of interviewing several leading ministers of the San Francisco Bay area regarding their Sunday evening services. One man let me know that, being only a student, I had no right to intrude on the time of such a busy and important man. Another insisted on telling me what a great man he was, which was not the subject I wanted discussed. But a third man, the greatest of them all, took me into his study and acted as if he had been honored by my coming. To think of him still lifts up my heart. Let us realize how easily we can lose our ability to sympathize with others and enter into their situations. May God protect us from the pride which is one of the hazards of our profession.

Finally, our pastoral ministry is limited by the extent of our own personal victories. The man who has himself known the hard way, but has been given the mastery through his Lord Jesus Christ, is the man who can help another. The worried, whining man need not be surprised if people hesitate in coming to him. Why should they consult a man who obviously knows no victory in his own life? It is still true that when men have been with Jesus there are unmistakable signs of his presence in their lives.

Yet one of the crosses we must bear is the assumption on the part of some people that the minister has never been subjected to the temptations they have faced, nor forced to carry the burdens placed on their shoulders. Sometimes it seems to me that if another person comes to me and begins, "Of course, you have never had to go through anything like this . . ." I'll not be able to stand it. A part of the healing is often a realization that a man's troubles are not unique and other men have borne them and still bear them. Arthur John Gossip says that after Stevenson had published several volumes of hope and joy, a certain Mr. Archer criticized the works as obviously the product of some sheltered man, protected from the grim realities of life. "Let this exasperatingly happy person have one touch of rheumatic fever," he concluded confidently, "and he will quickly change his tune." All the while Stevenson was suffering from sciatica, all but dead from hemorrhages, and his eyes were bandaged because of a serious disease. But he refused, as he said, to let the medicine bottles on his mantelpiece be the limit of his horizon, or the blood on his handkerchief be the chief fact in his life.[5]

When a man lives among his people with poise and assurance, the time will come when they will find help from him because of what he is. God always gives a golden extra to the man who has borne the battle bravely and finally conquered. Such a man always speaks with the voice of the Good Shepherd. Even his administration of the sacrament will mean more to the communicants because of his own spiritual qualities. The long pastorates are never matters of brilliant leadership only. They are possible because of the shining quality of the preacher's character.

Mrs. Humphrey Ward wrote to a member of parliament concerning a poor family in his district. The man had always sponsored social legislation and voted on the right side of all such issues. She was surprised, therefore, when he wrote to her, "I am so busy with plans for the race that I have no time for the individual." Mrs. Ward filed the letter away with this remark written across it: "Our Divine Lord, when last heard from, had not attained this sublime altitude." [6] God has called us to be servants of the Church, which is to say, servants of the people. We shall be saved from living in an unreal world of generalities if we learn how to be good pastors.

[5] Lichliter, *Whose Leaf Shall Not Wither*, Abingdon-Cokesbury, 1946, 40.

[6] Holman, *The Religion of a Healthy Mind*, Round Table Press, 1939.

4

The Evangelist

... do the work of an evangelist, make full proof of thy ministry.
II Timothy 4:5

W<small>E LIVE</small> in the kind of time that is productive of great religion. It is dangerous to draw the parallels too rigidly, for God breaks out in unexpected ways. But when we look at the creative periods of our religion in the past, they were always days of crisis and tension. A man who had a historical perspective would be more hopeful for a revival today than he would have been in the early part of this century. Then we were surfeited and satisfied with earthly trinkets, and our confidence in the future had not been shaken. Today we are dissatisfied and frightened. The most difficult mood for the Church to face is smugness, and whatever else we may be now, we are neither comfortable nor contented.

The paradox of the situation lies in our utter inability to feel secure, though Americans ought to feel more secure than any other people. We seem to be like men who have been given tremendous double-edged swords to wield, but are afraid to raise them lest we cut ourselves. In a hectic, futile attempt to find safety, the militarists spend more and more billions which create more and more fear. Even the materialist is beginning to ask what kind of security we are pursuing that simply makes the coming holocaust more terrible to contemplate for friend and

65

foe alike. Out of such conditions as these in days past, men turned toward the spiritual order and reached out for the eternal values.

Yet we languish in the midst of the wasteland without moving toward the springs. The very idea that there is a revival coming seems like foolish talk to many sincere, religious people. They can see no sign of it. There is nothing in their experience of the Church to provide any such hope. Most of their lives have been spent in being loyal to a movement that has no great power or compulsion. They are part of it out of habit, but they are hard put to give the outsider any compelling reason for coming into it. Except for the smaller sects which exist on revivals, most Christians have lost the belief that the Gospel has power to convert and redeem, and while it has a certain steadying influence, no doubt, they assume it would be poor taste and slightly indecent to expect it to break forth like a consuming fire. We may as well admit that the Church in our time has neither the revival hope nor the evangelistic expectation.

Our very idea of a successful church is an indication of how far we have departed from the evangelistic emphasis. The church is a success if it balances its budget, keeps up its property and has a minister who is acceptable in the community. Even Methodists, with their revival background and their passion for statistics, do not put the central emphasis on the number of people won for Christ, or on the number of children who have committed their lives to him. It would be a good thing for us to take stock of our changed standards and small aims. That there are many exceptions to this, I have no doubt, but that this is the general situation becomes increasingly, painfully apparent. The church which assumes that its first duty is to win souls is in a minority.

Some time ago one of our church colleges had a party in which folk dancing, or if you prefer, folk games, was a part of the program. A newspaper photographer took a picture of two attractive students dressed in costumes appropriate to Sadie Hawkins

Day. An anonymous letter came to me asking, "I wonder what John Wesley would have thought of this?" My guess is that he would not have been nearly so troubled by it as he would be concerned with the lack of evangelistic zeal among the people called Methodist. The revival which we know we must have if our world is to be saved, is prevented, first of all, by the absence of the evangelistic mood within the Church.

Outside the Church there is a barren skepticism concerning things religious which we have inherited from a past generation. We are still in the atmosphere which regards materialism as an adequate world view. We are still a part of the dogmatic scientism which differs from fundamentalism only in the object of its devotion. We are yet enthralled by a proud scientist's belief that science has made God unnecessary. Religion is still magic and ignorance to many contemporary persons. It is discouraging to note the little amount of thinking which has taken place in the religious field outside the Church. Many a modern has the vague belief that if things are to be any better it must be accomplished by any number of modern fads, but not by the Church.

It is a good thing, though not an encouraging thing, to talk about religion with people on trains and ships. It is not hard to talk about this subject, especially if you tell your companion you are a minister. This is a better beginning, I have discovered, than telling the person you are a bishop. Once started, you are in for it. You will hear about magic, miracle, quaint coincidence, moral pride and New Thought. You will seldom hear about Christianity as a way of life. You discover that for most people religion is a last resort. It is something they turn to in desperation when everything else has failed, with a doubting hope that maybe there is something in it after all. The average man has a mental block when it comes to accepting the Christian way. He is not so much opposed to it as he is cynical about it. The few sermons he has listened to in the last years have not set his imagination aflame, nor have they raised his estimate of what Christianity can do.

Religion may be organization, wealth, political pressure, pageantry or social service. It is not spiritual power. At its worst, it seems to him a pious racket, and at its best, it is making a vague gesture of approval in the direction of God.

Yet this man is not happy and self-sufficient. Far from it! He is not smugly satisfied. There are times when the lurking fear breaks into his consciousness and he would give anything for the faith which he remembers his father had. It has been a sad world since he lost God, but he does not know what makes it sad. He will believe the most impossible things if they are said by a scientist, but he cannot believe spiritual truth when spoken by the minister. As Hellenback said, "There is a scepticism which surpasses in imbecility the obtuseness of a clodhopper." [1]

Here, then, is our situation. Those who have it do not believe they have it, and those who need it most cannot recognize it. For the contemporary skepticism can only be dissolved in the fire of Christian fervor. The chief responsibility is with Christians, and the chief fault is ours. Once again we are in the position of the disciples who failed to heal the boy with the dumb spirit. But Jesus healed him, and when they asked the reason for their failure, he replied, "This kind can come forth by nothing, but by prayer and fasting" (Mark 9:29). If he should speak to us today, he would say that this evil spirit of cynicism cannot be removed but by the heat of religious fire and the power of Christian evangelism. In the meantime, we ought to look upon the fields white unto the harvest. We have talked too much about the difficulties of our task and too little about the opportunities before us. Pascal said, "Pity the atheist who seeks." Soon or late, the atheist has to seek, and while his search may not be according to knowledge, still his searching makes him vulnerable to the attack of the Gospel.

The revival has to begin among the preachers. This will bring some comfort to the laity, who often show a preference for it to

[1] Quoted by Carr, *op. cit.,* 51.

begin anywhere except in their own lives. But until we are ready to begin with ourselves, we are not ready to begin at all. This is the time when we ought to ask, "Lord, is it I?" Again let us examine our tendency toward double-mindedness. Is it not possible that our work has been full of darkness? Perhaps our eye can become single again if we think of ourselves as missionaries and the Church as a missionary institution. We are not to maintain, but to advance.

I. There is a Message

One of the reasons we have steered away from evangelism is that we have associated it with an uncouth, unprepared approach which takes refuge in loudly screaming certain phrases. There is a kind of emotionalism associated with some revivals which every cultured person properly resents. It is some consolation to know that this is not new. John Wesley protested against the same thing when he said:

> I am sick and tired of hearing some men preach Christ. Let but a pert, self-sufficient animal that hath neither sense nor grace, bawl out something about Christ or his blood, or justification by faith, and his hearers cry out, "What a fine gospel sermon!" [2]

This kind of preaching has done much harm for it has deepened the doubting of our time. We can hardly blame men for being repelled by this claptrap, and one of the hardest blows struck against the Church has been the number of such preachers who have managed to get on the radio.

The evangelistic message is not one marked by outgrown phraseology, but by directness of approach and appeal to the heart. A personal worker talked with a woman in a Boston hotel lobby about her need of Christ, and when he left, there were tears in her eyes. When her husband returned, he asked her what had

[2] Quoted by Luccock and Hutchinson, *op. cit.*, 18.

upset her. She told him of this strange man who had been speaking about her spiritual need. "Why didn't you tell him to mind his own business?" he asked. She answered, "If you had been here you would have thought it was his business." [3] When we have lost our self-consciousness in the service of our Lord, and when we have given ourselves with singleness of mind to the work, we can speak to all persons as that man spoke to the stranger in a hotel lobby.

Our message is centered in an event, which is to say, it is precise and specific. This is the difference between our message and the word of other religions. It is the difference between religion and philosophy. It is the difference between religion and secularism. As an English scholar once remarked, the decay of Christianity leads men "to make gods of their abstract nouns." The powerlessness of much of our preaching and much of our counseling lies in our abstractness. Every great recovery of Christianity has been a recovery of the concrete nature of our message and our experience. Martin Luther rebelled not only against the immoral practices of the medieval Church, but also against its man-centered state which had become vague about its source of salvation. He brought the Christian tradition back to its immediacy. Justification by Faith was a doctrine grounded in the Incarnation and offering redemption here and now. The Evangelical Revival in England was a return from the vagueness of Deism to the concreteness of Christianity.

One can read the speculations in the Christian field during these past years and note the same wandering away from center. For the word God, which means something tangible, we have turned to words like Drift, Ground, Principle, Tendency. For the coming of the Holy Spirit with power, we have preferred to talk about sublimating impulses and reforming inclinations. For Jesus Christ as Savior, we have substituted a wandering carpenter who

taught some good things and showed men a good example. All
of this has been a reflection of our lack of a faith anchored in a
particular event which took place at a particular time. When
this historical sense of Christianity departs from us, we lose its
power.

At the heart of the Christian story there is the insistence that
God acted, and we miss the whole meaning if we do not see that
the initiative was His. Whenever we lose this sense of a specific
act as the center of our message, it becomes vague and unconvinc-
ing. We are not to proclaim the love of God who in a general way
desires the best for everyone, but we proclaim the love of God
which was in Christ reconciling the world to Himself. This saves
us from pantheism and mysticism. It is this central event which
makes Christianity wonderful in its redeeming power, and the
attempt to make it anything else is a betrayal.

In our time we have seen what sick systems are produced when
we try to keep the Christian vocabulary without the central
Christian event. This is the cause of our poor, subjective, un-
healthy concern with our own emotions. This turns men in upon
themselves instead of taking them out of themselves, which is
always their real need. Woe unto a generation which departs
from John's magnificent insight: "And the Word was made
flesh . . ." (John 1:14). From the beginning, the dangerous
heresies of the Church have attacked this reality of the Incarnation. Sometimes they have made it an appearance only,
and at other times they have tried to make it secondary. God has
given the Church wisdom enough to resist these movements and
recognize them for what they are, but there are times when they
are so subtle that we do not attack them without equivocation
until it is almost too late. We are in such a period.

When a man tells us that he loves us and values us highly, we
are glad to hear it and it gives us a certain amount of satisfaction.
The political party which vaguely mentions the general welfare
in its platform may win the votes of those already committed to

its philosophy, yet it captures no new recruits. But if a man, at great cost to himself, performs a heroic act for us, that changes our lives. If a party makes life better for me without compromising its promises, I will give it my loyalty. So it is that God's act in Christ brings to me more than mere sentimentalism. It brings to me a new life because it brings me a vision of God acting on my behalf. We shall not evangelize the world until we get back to the centrality of the Incarnation and keep it at the center of everything we say.

Yet we are not mere admirers of a historical event. Ours is not ancestor worship. The miracle of the whole matter lies in this—that the ancient event is always happening and God's redemptive act in Christ is a present experience. The Incarnation is our contemporary. A man like Studdert-Kennedy saw the Crucifixion repeating itself on the battlefields of World War I. H. A. Hodges had the overwhelming assurance on an Oxford street that the Eternal had become his footman. And there have been times in my own poor life when the Divine Forgiveness has flooded my spirit with the same fresh intensity it must have manifested to men in the days of Jesus' earthly ministry. We had a phrase we used more often a generation ago—"personal savior." It meant that God in Christ still comes to each man directly; it signified the amazing truth that Calvary and Easter stand just outside each man's door. To every soul the Savior says, "Behold I stand at the door and knock"; to his mind he proclaims, "I am the way, the truth, and the life"; and to his heart he brings the quiet assurance, "He that hath seen me hath seen the Father."

George Jean Nathan, the dramatic critic, once described the work of a certain actress as the first Camille he had ever seen who had died of catarrh. It is not only on the stage that people turn tragic diseases into sniffles. Preachers sometimes treat the Cross the same way, by making it artificial, mechanical melodrama. By our lack of understanding we present it as much ado about very little. The cosmic significance of God having acted to redeem and ennoble men is made into some grotesque parable with no more power than a fable by Aesop. Let us make it as simple as we can, but let us not rob the Event of its majesty and awe by stripping all the divine mystery from it. It is hard to say which is worse—to treat it like some mechanical transaction unworthy of a second-rate Oriental chieftain, or to make it a weak and ineffectual parable. It was a Divine Event!

First of all, then, we must recover the message. We must get the sense of the unique word of our faith. We must be aware that God has given us the earnest of His concern to save us from sin and death. This is not just one philosophy of life among many others. This is the Good News!

II. I Am the Messenger

A tribe on Mount Hagen in New Guinea offered a gift to a missionary if he would take his God and depart. They said that while he was there they could not go on practicing their pagan customs. But some of the young men disagreed with the tribe's request. "It is impossible to send this God away again," they said. "He lives in our own hearts. As soon as we want to do something a voice asks whether it is right before God. And we don't want him to go away. We don't want to return to paganism." [4] To be entrusted with a message like that is a terrible responsibility, but it is also a mighty privilege. To be an evangelist is to be conscious of being entrusted with a saving word.

The men who have been most successful in winning men to Christ have had this sense of their divine commission and the potential power in the word they proclaimed. This is not the same thing as the egotism which characterizes many so-called successful preachers. It is the self-effacing assurance of men whose confidence is not in themselves but in their calling. John Wesley is one of the best examples. Listen to John Nelson's story

[4] *Man's Disorder and God's Design*, 184.

of how he was called to become one of Methodism's greatest
early lay preachers:

> Whitefield was to me as a man who could play well on an instru-
> ment, for his preaching was pleasant to me and I loved the man, . . .
> but I did not understand him. I was like a wandering bird cast out of
> its nest till Mr. John Wesley came to preach his first sermon at Moor-
> fields. . . . As soon as he got upon the stand, he stroked back his hair
> and turned his face toward where I stood, and, I thought, fixed his eyes
> upon me. His countenance fixed such an awful dread upon me, before
> I heard him speak, that it made my heart beat like the pendulum of
> a clock; and when he did speak, I thought his whole discourse was
> aimed at me. When he had done, I said, "This man can tell me the
> secrets of my heart; he hath not left me there; for he hath showed the
> remedy, even the blood of Jesus," . . . I durst not look up, for I
> imagined all the people were looking at me. Before Mr. Wesley con-
> cluded his sermon he cried out, "Let the wicked man forsake his way,
> and the unrighteous man his thoughts; and let him return unto the
> Lord, and he will have mercy upon him; and to our God, for he
> will abundantly pardon." I said, "If that be true, I will turn to God
> today." [5]

When a preacher is aware that he has such a word for each man
in the congregation, there is some hope that he will be more than
a pleasant speaker on religious themes. He will be an evangelist.

I am convinced that for many of us the most necessary thing to
do just now is recapture the wonder of having been called to be
ministers of Christ. Paul's ministry was replenished constantly by
this humbling and inspiring recollection:

> Unto me, who am less than the least of all saints, is this grace given,
> that I should preach among the Gentiles the unsearchable riches of
> Christ. (Ephesians 3:8)

What a sad thing it is when a man loses the glory of the fact that
he was "made a minister." There is a supernatural element in it

---

[5] Luccock and Hutchinson, *op. cit.*, 98.

which makes the ministry terrible yet glorious in its responsibility.

What we might have been, without the safety of the ministry's discipline, ought to come home to us not once but many times. None of us is what he ought to be nor what he has high hopes of becoming. Yet we cannot but give solemn thanks for having been granted grace to hear the summons to the Kingdom. If perchance we have lost this or forgotten it, we may find our effectiveness increased manyfold by its recovery. The minister is well employed in recounting what he owes to Christ.

Not the least of the great experiences of the ministry is the sense of belonging to a glorious company. Our job has to be at times a lonesome one, but the minister who thinks of himself as a star called upon to play an isolated, spectacular role, misunderstands the nature of his work. There has been too much of that among Protestant preachers. We are individualists, it is true, but we go wrong if we think we can divorce our ministries from the fellowship. As an English preacher put it:

The very idea of an isolated Christian, that a person can be a Christian on his own, is the myth of degenerate Protestantism; just as the idea that the Church and the Kingdom are one is the myth of a degenerate Catholicism.[6]

We belong to one another and we have responsibilities to one another. Every man's success enriches me and every man's failure is my own.

There is not enough virtue in the best of us to make our lives too important in themselves. Our meaning is derived from the things we stand for and the values we symbolize. A man's ministry may be regarded by a large number of people as a successful one. Yet how quickly a man is forgotten after he is gone and how relentlessly the procession marches on. How quickly an isolated success is brought low and how little is really accomplished by the man whose eye has been on the main chance. No, only to the

6 Davies, *op. cit.*, 77.

extent that we are aware of ourselves as servants of the Church and messengers of the King do we find eternal life now and forever. A greater man than any of us spoke the necessary word about our speaking: "For we preach not ourselves, but Christ Jesus the Lord; and ourselves your servants for Jesus' sake" (II Corinthians 4:5).

It is a strange and ridiculous situation that, in the day when every cheap and degrading product and cause is using every method possible to influence people, the Christian ministry should be so fearful of persuading men by means of an emotional appeal. We timidly skirt around the edge of a direct aim for decisions, under the illusion that valid choices are made only in the atmosphere of a cold intellectualism. What nonsense! Men act when they are emotionally stirred, and if God has given man the gift of eloquence, He certainly meant it to be used for winning men to Christ as well as for selling motor cars. We are afraid to aim straight for a verdict and as a result the vague stirrings of the spirit are kept weak and ineffectual. The evangelist is not preaching something he dreamed up or created. He has been sent to say something for God and anything less than the full power of his persuasion is an insult to the One who sent him. Let us have done with this lifeless arguing. We ought not to assume that only the sects are commissioned to set running the high tide of emotional power.

In his recollections, Dr. Mott has recalled a student conference presided over by Moody some sixty years ago. They met for a month with only one meeting a day, the rest of the time being spent in study and prayer. Moody wanted one hundred men for foreign missionary service, and at the beginning of the conference only three men were committed. But by the last day the ninety-ninth man had decided, and at the concluding prayer service, the hundredth man came forward.[7] In our time we would

[7] Neill in *Renewal and Advance,* edited by Ranson, Edinburgh House Press, 1948, 82.

have said this was high pressure. But if we had the sense of being God's messengers called to invite men to enlist under His banner, we would feel that our job was only half begun until we had used all our powers of persuasion to win men for full-time service. Perhaps as much as anything, we need to recover the sense of our status as divine messengers of the Highest.

III. There is a Terrible Urgency

With the world under the threat of atomic weapons, it acts like a club of elderly women making futile gestures but without power to make one decisive action. We flutter about vainly hoping that time will take care of it. The Church, faced with the responsibility of mustering big spiritual guns, remains "a nominal church" which is another way of saying an empty ecclesiastical shell. Our way of administering the Balm of Gilead has no chance against the Bomb of Hiroshima. We have been content for so long to hold our own that our whole psychology is negative. We know how to defend but we have forgotten how to attack.

The Church today has many competitors, it is true, but its chief obstacle is its own fearfulness and lack of concern. In some of the most difficult fields in the nation there are churches full of throbbing life, which indicates that the revival waits only until we are ready to launch it. I do not think the whole fault lies with the laymen. There are many churches where the laymen are ready for a great forward movement of evangelism but the minister hesitates. Churches surrounded by people who are as sheep without a shepherd confine their programs to the small horizons of visionless leaders. God is ready to break out on the land, but the instrument He would use is dull and ineffectual.

Dr. Burton said in his Yale lectures on preaching:

It has been the sin of my life that I have not always taken aim. I have been a lover of subjects. If I had loved men more, and loved subjects only as God's instrument of good for men, it would have been better and I should have more to show for my labor under the sun.[8]

Probably most of us fall under that indictment more or less. We have been content to discuss matters of general import rather than go direct to each man with the urgent word of the Gospel. Evangelistic preaching has a "Thou art the man" quality about it. There is a kind of hurry in it as if the time were short and the decision must not be delayed. The aim is not to put men in a meditative mood, but to put them under an immediate conviction. This is not to say that it is bad for men to have good things to think about or that a preacher is doing nothing when he enlarges the interests of the congregation. But when the house is burning, that is not the time to study the history of fire-fighting apparatus. That is the time to turn the stream on the flames and, if necessary, beat them out with your own hands. The man in the congregation is caught in his dilemma now, and if he is to be saved, now is the time. The whole spirit of the day creates that tense atmosphere now and thus prepares the way for our direct and immediate word.

Our task is not merely to convey certain ideas to the people. It is not primarily to get them to join an organization. It is rather to introduce them to Christ that his new reality may work a sudden transforming miracle. Perhaps we need a rebirth of faith that the spirit of Christ can still transform human life. We need less confidence that the only way is our way and more willingness that God should do it His own way. We need at the same time to be more urgent in bringing men to Christ and less anxious to make them our kind of Christians. Again the word of the Apostle speaks to us:

Who then is Paul, and who is Apollos, but ministers by whom ye believed, even as the Lord gave to every man? I have planted, Apollos

[8] Quoted by Powell, *op. cit.*, 81.

watered; but God gave the increase. So then neither is he that planteth any thing, neither he that watereth; but God that giveth the increase. (I Corinthians 3:5–7)

To put it another way, we need to be more concerned with bringing men directly to Christ and less concerned with what he may wish to do with them afterward.

The world is a battleground of fighting faiths where victory goes to the one which believes its time has come. There was never much accomplished by men with no sense of immediate urgency. If we are unaware of the present danger we are mere passive elements in the struggle. The world is affected by the movements which see themselves as made to conquer in such a time as this. These recent years have shown us the latent power in Christianity when it has a sense of now or never. It is also apparent that a Christianity dedicated to a gradual passiveness can be pushed aside without much effort. The Gospel at its best has a sense of "the latter days." This is not to say that we must be apocalyptists in the traditional sense, but we must be aware that when God acts the Great Day has arrived. The evangelist is aware of the terrible issues at stake at this very moment when the decision is being made.

A Chinese bishop was examining his devastated diocese at the close of the war with Japan. He was not nearly so disturbed as might have been expected. "If we have got the Living Church," he said, "it is easy to put up the buildings." [9] And when things are alive, they are vibrant with immediate expectation. We can put up the buildings, as we are doing in America, and that is good. There is no virtue in working with inadequate facilities. But let us not confuse the putting up of buildings with renewing the life of the Church. That can happen only when the Church is aware of its responsibility to redeem men's lives now and knows that God will make its strength sufficient for the task.

[9] *Man's Disorder and God's Design*, I, 111.

IV. Our Joyful Opportunity

There is no joy to compare with the evangelist's. A man never loses the happiness of his calling if he is winning men to Christ. He can put up with many disappointments and go through many a sore trial without surrender if he is introducing men to his Lord. But the other successes of the ministry will not long compensate for lack of evangelistic success. We were not meant to be promoters or administrators or purchasing agents, though we must do something in each of these fields. We were meant to be the bringers of good tidings to disappointed men. We are called to offer the Balm of Gilead for sin-sick souls.

We must be seekers. Ours is the shepherd's task, which is not only to find the lost, but to help men know they are lost. Over and against the so-called "down and outer" there is the "up and outer." We have erred in assuming that only those who work with the poor and the unlovely are called to be evangelists. Perhaps those who are in greatest need of a shepherd today are the men with great resources and little purposes. I heard a minister say to a wealthy man one time, "Why don't you give up all the silly things you think you have to do because of your position, and dedicate your life to the service of Christ?" I saw the astonishment on his face that any man would dare speak to him so directly. I saw the time when those words bore fruit and the man's life was changed. One of the greatest regrets of my life is that there has come to me a vast number of such opportunities, and my word was not spoken. We are too timid.

Our evangelism will not always be a matter of rescuing someone who has gone astray. It will be also the great work of preventing men from taking the wrong turning and making the wrong decision. We are not unmindful of Jesus' word:

I say unto you, that likewise joy shall be in heaven over one sinner that repenteth, more than over ninety and nine just persons, which need no repentance. (Luke 15:7)

But this is not to minimize the significance of the just person. It is to make clear how valuable every single soul is in the sight of God. The hope of the world lies in those "just persons" who give their strength to the weak and their example to the wavering.

There is a poem about a community which was diligent in keeping an ambulance on duty at all times, at the foot of a dangerous cliff. When it was suggested that it might be wiser to build a fence along the edge of the cliff and prevent the accidents from happening, the idea was greeted with scorn. Why build a fence when the ambulance was kept on duty? Let us not fall into that trap in our evangelism. The prevention of the tragedy may be less spectacular and perhaps only God will know about it, but it may be more productive for the Kingdom.

Evangelism is the awakening of men to their own worth and possibilities. The world has a way of drugging men until they are no longer aware of what they are. Salvation is often a matter of learning who we are. We can play our sordid parts and convince ourselves that we are smart and modern, until some simple, direct person says, "But it is sordid." In a homiletical magazine there appeared this quotation:

Longfellow could take a worthless sheet of paper, write a poem on it, and make it worth $6,000—there is genius.

Rockefeller can sign his name to a piece of paper, and make it worth millions—that is capital.

Uncle Sam can take gold, stamp an eagle on it, and make it worth $20—that is money.

A mechanic can take material worth $5 and make an article worth $20—that is skill.

An artist can take a 50-cent piece of canvas, paint a picture on it, and make it worth $1,000,000—that is art.

God can take a worthless, sinful life, wash it in the blood of Christ, put His spirit into it and make it a blessing to humanity—that is salvation.[10]

[10] From *The Tie*.

There is no greater joy than to be used by God in the working of His transforming miracles.

For the cowards we offer power. For the selfish we are voices of self-releasing duty. For cheapness we come to offer nobility and recall men to their state as children of the King. Ours is the weight to throw in the balance when a man wavers "Twixt muck and a golden crown," as Studdert-Kennedy phrased it. All of this means that we are called to enter into the joy of our Lord, for no man is given the privilege of sharing so completely in the creative triumph of God, as is the evangelist.

Dr. George MacLeod of the Iona Community in Scotland was visited by a Clydeside working man enamored with the gospel of Marx. Finally the man burst out: "You folk have got it; if only you knew that you had it, and if only you knew how to begin to say it." Dr. David A. MacLennan, who told the story, commented on it by saying, "Please God, we shall master the art of saying it. . . ." We shall learn how to say it, when we believe it is true. When we note what Communists can do with their poor, one-sided, sentimental drivel, we ought to be ashamed of ourselves at the way we have used the greatest news the world ever heard. We ought to shout for joy that in such a day as this we are Christian evangelists.

5

The Revealer

Blessed art thou . . . for flesh and blood hath not revealed it unto thee, but my Father which is in heaven. MATTHEW 16:17.

HOWEVER critically we may regard Peter's confession of Jesus' Messiahship, we can hardly doubt its central significance so far as the Church is concerned. Christianity was possible only after Jesus was recognized as having a cosmic meaning. You can have a party or a sect built on some good man's observations and example, but you cannot have a religion until you have a life that is a revelation of God. This is something that men easily forget and try to ignore. But their little efforts to transform our faith into a moralism built on a good man's teaching always come to naught. We may phrase it differently in different generations, but Christianity stands on its affirmation: "Thou art the Christ, the Son of the living God" (Matthew 16:16).

Now it is most important to note Jesus' insistence that this knowledge was a revealed knowledge. It did not come from human effort alone. It was not merely a matter of reasoning through, but a vision which illuminated Peter's mind, and it came from God. It would be dangerous to carry this single incident too far in our interpretations, but surely we are on safe ground when we observe Jesus' affirmation that ultimate meanings come not by rational processes but by revelation. The experience the disciples had with their Master was necessary and yet it was in a sense preparatory. They had come to know him as a man, and a great teacher. But they saw his universal meaning when God revealed it to them.

This is something we are in constant danger of minimizing. Enamored with the enormous potentialities in the research method, we often consider it the only way to understanding. There seems to be no limit to the piling up of facts and the increasing of knowledge if we will patiently use our minds to experiment and gather data. When we surrender completely to this spirit, we play down the importance of the ultimate questions because they are embarrassments to the scientific method. Gradually the spiritual and emotional life of man is whittled away until all of our life is seen in terms of rational processes. This goes on until a banished emotional nature insists on coming back, oftentimes in an uncontrolled rebellion against the intellectual and reasonable. The result is an outburst of crude antireason which works havoc with both its champions and their opponents.

We may live with the facts and get acquainted with the "laws of nature." We may learn how to deal with the physical environment and work the marvels which make life complicated and physically comfortable. But there comes a time when an outraged spiritual nature will no longer be silent. Then we hunger for something our cleverness cannot discover and our minds are twisted with frustration and fear. For man does not live by knowledge alone, and he has a terrible hunger for meaning. But meaning does not fit into the test tube and subject itself to chemical analysis. It is when something beyond reason cries out for exploration and we do not know how to go farther, that madness captures our minds.

Now Jesus simply assumes that, if men live close to God, He will tell them about the finalities and the meanings. Flesh and blood will not do it because the physical soon reaches a barrier beyond which it cannot go. Then there comes the whisper from above, deep in the heart of man. Then there bursts on the spirit a vision of the Holy City toward which we are moving. Then the Father visits the children with a word about the far country and a hint concerning human destiny. When a man has been visited by this divine insight, he establishes a new outpost for the race and humanity says of him, "Blessed art thou."

The eternal conflict between the humanists and the theists is in this realm. Many a man who refuses to believe in a personal God, believes in the adequacy of human knowledge as a basis for salvation. He will insist that we find the necessary truth by the same process we use in the attaining of all knowledge; that truth waits for us to discover it and we simply use our intellects to plod patiently forward until we find it. In this approach there is no room for a God who reveals meaning. If He exists at all, He is regarded as passive and impersonal. His function is to hold things together and keep the laws in operation, and beyond that He will not go. Men, therefore, must gird themselves for the difficult task of seeking and experimenting until they arrive at workable spiritual meanings.

But the theist differs with his humanist brother at this point of defining the nature of God. The Christian, for example, cannot believe that the Father of Jesus Christ is inactive in His relations to men and the world. If we must use our gifts and dedicate our energies to this high task of spiritual discovery, still the Christian has the belief that our desire to seek is the gift of God. When we see through a glass darkly, yet see enough to fill our hearts with singing, He illuminates our vision. The hunger to know more is God's doing, and the insights of the saints and the prophets are His promptings. The difficulty of finding is not because He desires to hide the secrets from us, nor His inability or refusal to help us in our search. The difficulty is a terrible blindness which afflicts us after we have looked too long and too hard at the world's glitter. It is due to our sin and our wandering.

When a man has been found by Christ, he has the feeling that he was the object of a long search which would have failed without an infinite patience on his Lord's part. We cannot but believe he is more anxious to teach us than we are to learn. He desires us to find, more than we desire to seek. In short, the Christian experience is redeeming, precisely because it takes us into the presence of the God who sought us even while we were yet sinners. Revelation is not so much our seeking as it is God's seeking. He is not only ready but He is terribly anxious for us to enter into the secrets of His nature.

For this greatest of experiences, it is the humble heart more than the clever mind that is necessary. Truth is hidden from wise and prudent men but revealed unto babes. This is not because God despises wisdom and prudence, but simply that the wise get tangled up in their own conceits and are blinded by their pride. These are the walls which He will not penetrate, for the revelation, to mean anything, has to be freely given and freely appropriated.

We are moving into the holy of holies when we speak of the minister as a revealer. Dare we assume that our ministry shall be a revelation to our people? Does any man have the right to expect that in his own person God may reveal His will and purpose to other men? This is dangerous territory to explore, for the moment we begin to get a Messiah-complex, we are undone. But the history of the Church is the story of plain men whose eyes were opened to the mystery of God's will. There seems no reason to believe that we have come to the end of that possibility, and there is no reason to doubt God's continued willingness to reveal Himself to men through other men. If this seems too high for our aim, still we cannot escape the implications of our calling. We are called to be the kind of men God can use to make plain His meaning.

I. Some Misapprehensions

Once the idea of revelation has been adopted as possible, and indeed, as inevitable, we are in grave danger of making it too

irrational and too far removed from human experience. This is
what the fundamentalist and sometimes the Neo-orthodox tend to
do. Quite properly the liberals and the theological humanists
protest against such a viewpoint, for it raises more questions than
it answers and it gives us a hopelessly dualistic world. Following
this path we arrive at a view of revelation which makes it something falling down into history and human experience from the
outside, with no relation whatsoever to human experience and
human thinking. This is the way which leads to narrow dog-
matism, authoritarianism, and a neurotic religion.

Now and again we find a minister who has taken this way and
now believes himself to be the divine dispenser of God's directions. He withdraws from the fellowship of the Church and
opposes its programs. He has entered into that frightful state of
believing himself the only one to whom God has revealed Himself. He does not hesitate to go against all human knowledge and
he denies the legitimacy of the scholars' insight. Strangely
enough, his revelation is seldom of a positive kind, but nearly
always a command to attack some differing Christian group and
carry his followers back to an ancient orthodoxy. His only salvation would lie in a recognition that truth is one and God does not
reveal anything contrary to it. It is a matter of believing that he
who is not against us is for us. Revelation does not contradict
human experience and rational processes, but supplements them
and uncovers the larger purposes of which they are a necessary
part.

Sometimes a man takes revelation as a substitute for hard
digging and careful study. The seminary student who prefers to
pray rather than to prepare his lesson is the kind of minister who
will be much attracted to the idea of revealed knowledge as a
substitute for earned knowledge. A great deal of what passes for
inspiration in some circles is laziness. The man who has not been
willing to pay the price for an education may play down its importance. He may insist that God will give things needful without

any effort if he is only properly pious. Yet experience in this field indicates that the vision comes after long hours of toil. There is nothing in the New Testament to encourage an idea of revelation as a substitute for effort. As a matter of fact, Paul is rather suspicious even of the ecstatic experience of speaking with tongues when it does not edify the brethren.

In one of his sermons, Dr. Edgar DeWitt Jones tells of the boy who came to a sage with a bird covered up in his hands. He said, "You are a very wise man and I come to you with this opportunity of proving it to the village. In my hand is a bird. Tell me, is it dead or alive?" If the man answered dead, he would open his hand and let it fly away. But if he answered alive, then the boy would crush it. But the wise old man gave an unexpected reply. "It is as you will," he said. And God deals with men in that same way. He does not disregard or override the human will and character. The great word does not come to the small man, and the penetrating insight is not given to the shallow spirit.

There is no effortless, magical foretelling in the religious concept of revelation. The prophet was no mere fortune teller, yet the prophet had visions and dreams. He could say, "Thus saith the Lord." But his authoritative word was always conditioned by the kind of man he was and it was always affected by his previous experience. I sat one Sunday in a service listening to a preacher with an affected voice which irritated me. He seemed to be pronouncing *history* as if the accent were on the middle syllable. Then it came to me that he was not using the word *history* but he was referring to *his story*. You can see the similarity and the difference. It entered my mind then that the prophets thought of *history* as *His story,* and that their understanding of its purposes and its nature rested on that fundamental revelation. This, in a sense, is the clue to the Christian understanding of history and it makes the Christian prophet not a supernatural predicter, but a spiritual man with insight.

The apocalyptic literature has a great fascination for men with a mechanical concept of revelation. How they glory in magical numbers, hidden calculations, and outlines of a determined future. The saddest part of the whole business is not in the charts they draw nor in the time wasted in making contemporary events fit the ancient patterns, but in the complete misunderstanding of the nature of our God and His relation to the world. It would seem that a simple understanding of their own human experience and some little inkling as to the significance of their religious experience would serve to dispel this nonsense. If religion is life, then it is not something which contradicts life nor is it something which denies human experience. We must guard against regarding revelation as an escape from this world into another world which exists only in our imaginations. There is another world, but it has the same Lord as this one. We cannot believe that all of our experience here is of no value so far as that next world is concerned. On the contrary, we feel that eternal life does begin here, and our subjection to the natural laws is a necessary spiritual discipline.

We must insist also that revelation is not to be regarded as something belonging only to a certain type of person or group. Anything that suggests the "superman" theory in religion is of the devil. We can hardly escape this conclusion when we read the Bible, for it has been the stones rejected by the worldly builders which have become the heads of the corner. It has been to the humble, the disinherited, the untrained, that God has appeared. Indeed, the Bible seems to be suspicious of the overeducated as if that process dulls apprehensions of divine truth.

The Church has had to fight against this aristocratic heresy since the beginning. There seems to be a kind of person who cannot believe that ordinary men can see God. There are supposed to be secrets too deep for ordinary minds to penetrate and a special knowledge which only a chosen few can attain. There are some who would, if they could, establish a religiously aristocratic caste, to whom the rank and file must pay allegiance and give obedience. One of the earliest groups of this kind was the Gnostics, and there runs through the early Epistles the threat which they expressed and the danger which they represented. Their idea would have transformed the Church into a secret society with gradations of excellence. If they had ever had their way, the Christian fellowship would have resembled the classes in a Hindu society.

Such groups are always with us and the danger they represent is never ended. In our time we have the people who despise the Church and gather a chosen few to go deeper into the hidden secrets of Christianity. They are looking for specially gifted people to join them. They would like to enlist "key" men. The motley crowd which surrounded Jesus would not be welcome in their meetings. It is doubtful if the disciples could have gained admittance. There is revelation, these people seem to say, but it is for us and not for you. It is something too hard for the ordinary man and too complicated for the average mind.

We must not, of course, assume that every man is the spiritual equal of every other man. Far from it! But we must assume that every man is potentially capable of receiving the revelation of God and we must be prepared to find such men in the most unexpected places. The minister will do well to listen to his people, especially to the ones who are not given to much talking and are not anxious to be heard. How often have I caught a flash of truth from the simple remark of some person who had no prominence. The memories of quiet communion with the humble saints are among the most precious we shall have. God seems ready to bring forth His truth out of unexpected places and under unexpected circumstances. The kind of man most gifted for this holy task is seldom the one most honored by the world.

Let us, therefore, be suspicious of any revelation which seems to be independent of ordinary men and their experience. Let us have many doubts concerning the revelation which claims to be of God but contradicts our knowledge. Let us be wary concerning the revelation which is denied to all men and possessed by a small group. Let us suspect the revelation which claims too much or assumes a complete understanding of the whole world. Justice Holmes in another connection has a word of warning for us here:

No philosopher can give you more than a world-poem. If he does not contradict experience or demand extravagant assumptions, and his construction hangs together, he has done all one can ask in reason. No system of the universe can be proved: there is nothing outside to prove it by. The fatal snare of system-makers is looking on the universe as a jigsaw puzzle. When they have taken it to pieces and put it together again, as they think (generally they have not), they think their way must be right; but at best they have dissected only one of its innumerable aspects (or fragments of incongruous aspects).[1]

That same criticism can be applied to many a religious specialist's system which he thinks came by revelation.

II. THE NATURE OF REVELATION

We shall go wrong in our attempt to understand the meaning of revelation if we approach it in any piecemeal fashion. Much of the false understanding of it and the false systems of religion raised on the false foundation have been due to a partial concept of religion itself. We must never lose sight of our faith as a total way of life. That would mean that it does not deal with special parts of human experience only. It does not appropriate special subjects for its treatment nor assume that only certain interests are amenable to its authority. God is the God of all life, and hence all life must be regarded as capable of revealing His nature and purpose. There is a sense, therefore, in which every experience is a revelation of God. Our minds are revelations of Him and our rational ability is simply His gift to think thoughts

[1] Howe, *Holmes-Pollock Letters,* Harvard University Press.

after Him. We believe that if any man thinks very long or very profoundly about any experience, it will lead him to God.

Now when that happens, our minds are enlightened in a special way. The man who has followed the glimmer of revelation in the ordinary event is led into the more adequate illumination of God's presence. He is in a position to have much more revealed to him because he has mounted to a higher plane. It is something like a detective, who first of all finds one small clue which gives him the needed hint as to the direction he must move. Then he finds another and another until at last he is in a position for the whole case to be made clear. Every clue is an added help in making him able to discover the final and all-revealing clue. Looking back on the path he has followed, he sees at last that there were a hundred little indications of the truth, if he could have seen them. In fact, all of his experience was trying to tell him the truth, if he had been able to understand. Which is to say: "Revelation is given chiefly through events to minds enlightened to receive it." [2]

The event, however, without the mind to appreciate it, does not reveal much. Just as the clue without the detective to read it and interpret it is useless, so the happening has to have a mind divinely illumined to see and understand. A true religious experience is the beginning of the creation of such a mind. It is not that a man has had something happen to him which will set him apart from life, but something has happened which will give him true insight into life. Conversion is the creation of a mind able to appreciate the will of God. God's problem, if we may put it like that, is to lead men to the place where they are able to appreciate the events which are telling what He has in mind. For the process is never complete until there is the event and a person present to receive the revelation.

---

[2] Temple, *Nature, Man and God,* Macmillan, 1949, 318. This great book has the most satisfiyng discussion of the nature of revelation I have found.

It would seem, therefore, that God must be anxious to have men who have eyes to see and ears to hear. There runs through the New Testament the sorrow of Jesus at the obtuseness of his followers and the insensitiveness of all men. He seems to be saying that it is all before us if we were not childishly engaged in silly pastimes which prevent our seeing it. There are sorrow and despair in his heart as he looks upon the stubborn insistence of his people to go toward destruction rather than to follow the way which was so obvious to him. However we may interpret the Atonement, we must see it was God's ultimate effort to reveal Himself to men. We can hardly doubt His love when we think of the patience it takes to put up with the selfish blindness and the proud stupidity of His children.

The minister is called upon to be an interpretor of God's revelation. The special event may be a warning or it may be an invitation. But without a man to proclaim its meaning, it will be ignored or misunderstood by many. The essential question is, what signifies this special experience which has just happened to me? What is the meaning of the political event or the open clash? What is God doing? To uncover the meanings in events is the task of the Christian preacher. He does not stand on the mountaintop apart. He is in the midst of the difficulty and he brings to it the light of Christian experience and a word which makes clear what was only dimly known.

The man who would be an instrument in the hands of his Lord to reveal the will of God must consecrate himself, which is another way of saying he must discipline himself. If we have advanced farther than other men into the spirit of the Gospel, we shall be in a position to see the meanings of human experience more clearly. We learn to read the signs more easily and our words can be spoken with more authority. The Indians called buzzards "tracks in the skies." To the unskilled man the tracks meant nothing and would not even be observed. But to the disciplined woodsman, they told a great deal. God, too, is often tracks in the skies, and if our spirits are able to appreciate the signs, we can be revealers.

I have gone through the countryside with a naturalist and learned how blind I was. We may examine a rocky hill with a geologist and learn so much from so little, that we marvel at the way the rocks tell their secrets to the man who understands them. The purpose of art appreciation in the schools is to train people to become capable of entering into the experience which the artist has prepared for them. It is as if all the inanimate things in nature are shouting to us their wonderful secrets, but only a few have cared enough to learn their language. There are a few people who will insist that there is nothing there to learn, simply because they cannot understand. But most of us gladly sit at the feet of the men who have spent their lives in learning how to speak the language of science, geology, music, art. And many of us learn that, while we may not have the gift of the genius, we have enough ability to listen and believe.

We must insist again, however, that we are not speaking of something belonging to only the chosen few. It belongs to all men but not all will follow the discipline. They will be too busy with other things, or too skeptical to learn. We should have a right to expect, it would seem to me, that the ministry would become as competent in spiritual affairs as the experts in the fields of art and science. " Every good artist," said Leonardo da Vinci, "has two subjects—man and the hopes of his soul." For the minister, when he is in his role of revealer, there are two subjects also—God's ways, and how to make them plain.

R. C. Hutchinson, the English novelist, in discussing the absence of stature noticeable in much modern fiction, said:

The splendor possible in fiction will never come, I think, except from discovering in every human (good or bad, intelligent or idiotic) a value far higher than that which he derives from having, in the last few hundred millennia, come to surpass the lower animals in sentience and understandings: an individual and unique value, acquired from an extra-natural source.[3]

It is this fundamental Christian belief which makes revelation so important. Man is the only creature capable of receiving it and understanding it. The man who can contribute something in this field is the true servant of God and man.

III. Its Boundaries

A great deal of the suspicion concerning revelation has been due to the involved speech of those who would reveal the inner secrets of mystical experience. Stuart Chase quotes a paragraph from a social scientist, and out of kindness withholds the source:

In conformity with the preceding point, if all the interacting parties (in marriage, in minority-majority groups, in different occupational, religious, political, economic, racial, ethnic, and other interacting groups and persons) view the given overtly similar (or dissimilar) traits: A, B, C, D, N (physical, biological, mental, socio-cultural) as negligible values or as no values at all, as comprising even no similarity (or dissimilarity), such overt similarities-dissimilarites are innocuous in the generation of either solidarity or antagonism.[4]

This sounds like the high-flown verbiage of some religious specialists. You find such talk in some of the mystics and in *Science and Health.* One turns to the simplicity of the New Testament with fresh appreciation.

But while revelation is a thing of plain speech, it does not come to us in trivialities. People who go all out for guidance so often seem to assume that the Almighty has nothing better to do than save them from minor inconveniences. One man insisted in my presence that it had been revealed to him that if he made a

[3] Hutchinson, "If One Must Write Fiction," *Saturday Review of Literature,* August 3, 1949.
[4] Chase, *The Proper Study of Mankind,* Harper, 1948, 44.

certain business call the man would not be home. Sure enough, he found out later the man was out at that particular time. If being sensitive to God's will results in such trivial matters, then it seems a shabby thing and hardly worth our serious consideration. The greatest doubt in my mind concerning spiritualism's claim to contact the dead is in the silly signs it often holds up for proof. Surely the moving of tables and the tapping on floors is not the kind of thing a departed, eternal spirit would do. It makes the other world a place where there is nothing worth while happening. Revelation has to do with destiny and eternity. It is not some new fad for the dilettante to experiment with nor is it to be regarded as a minor hobby for those desiring to experiment with the occult.

The man who is capable of receiving the revelation of God is not a man who has had superhuman knowledge bestowed on him. When men get into difficulty, they would like some angel to fly to their rescue. Ministers, being human, are often tempted to claim they know more than they do. They sometimes take more authority than they have any right to claim. With the best of intentions, we can allow our enthusiasm to run away with our judgment. We can overlook our own limitations and justify the ways of God to men, as if we were supermen. It may well be that the time will come when we may see the vision of God, but if that happens to us, it will be too bad if we use it as an excuse to speak like oracles on every occasion. It will be much better if, like an ancient prophet who saw the Lord high and lifted up, we cry out: "Woe is me! for I am undone; because I am a man of unclean lips, and I dwell in the midst of a people of unclean lips; for mine eyes have seen the King, the Lord of hosts" (Isaiah 6:5). Stubborn, prideful men have a way of twisting their visions to suit their own conveniences. They do great harm. Arthur Balfour said, "I am more or less happy when being praised, not very uncomfortable when being abused, but I have moments of uneasiness when being explained." I should imagine that God has many such moments of uneasiness.

IV. THE PROMISE

To know God and be aware to some extent of His plans gives to men the necessary background and framework for their living. There used to be training centers for the monks, and one was given an interesting task. He went through the library, the orchard or the stable and put his hand on each man's shoulder with the simple word: "Why are you doing this? Don't forget God." The world is always in need of men who will do that task. To every person He speaks His word and asks His question. He reveals the meaning of the small task in the framework of the Eternal's plan. He brings each man's attention to ultimate things and to divine truths. Truly, the man who has lived in such a way as to appreciate God's meaning in the events of his life is in a position to help others feel the tug of the Unseen.

There is a fine passage in a contemporary novel. Before the Battle of Hastings, the Bishop speaks to the defending English army. Here is the description of his speaking:

Bishop Wulfstan preached that night so that men's hearts were stirred within them. Though he had ever had the grace of words, no one had heard him speak as in that hour. He used not his own thoughts but those of the great fathers of his nation, clothing them anew with brighter glory, as though he showed forth all the holiness, wisdom and beauty garnered in England since Augustine's days. To every man it seemed that for the first time he beheld his heritage.[5]

Something of this is the high privilege of the preacher. We let men see their heritage and their homeland. Revelation is to make plain who we are and from whence we have come. It is to enlarge our minds, and deepen our spirits.

[5] Muntz, *The Golden Warrior*, Scribner's, 1949, 286.

The whole Christian history is a revelation of God, and if we know it well, we can bring its enlightenment into every dark situation. We dare to believe that, in the story of Jesus and the history of the Church, we see the pivotal clues. Christians have had that sense of revelation in their tradition from the beginning. That is what makes Christian creeds so different from our modern ideas of what a creed ought to be. We assume that when we repeat a creed, we are simply saying what we believe and what we have sworn to maintain. But the Christian Creeds, and noticeably the Nicene and Apostles' Creeds, consist of a recital of the mighty acts of God in Christ and His Church. Christian revelation never deals with abstractions but with definite actions of God. One cannot but be aware of all the defects of the Church. No one is more aware of those defects than we who are its ministers, for our own defects, so obvious to us, are also a part of what we offer the Church. But after all has been said that can be said, still it remains true that the Church is the one institution whose history is a proclamation and a revelation of God's nature and purpose in the redeeming Cross and Resurrection of Jesus Christ.

The tragedy of human life so often lies in its vision of truth coming too late. A contemporary play [6] gives the sad story of a man with good intentions who fumbles away his chances for dignity by relying on "being well liked." He allows his two boys to build their futures on cheating and laziness. The time comes when what others have known for a long time becomes clear to him. He realizes at last that he has always been a failure trying to hide it with pretense. Then he commits suicide so that his wife will have enough money to make the last payment on their home when there is no longer anyone left who really wants to live in it. If only, we say, that man could have had the real meanings of life revealed to him. If only he could have known who he was and what he was made for. Not the least of the joys of the minis-

[6] Miller, *The Death of a Salesman.*

try is the high honor of bringing into confused lives the revelation of Christ.

The high calling of being a source of revelation and an interpreter of God demands a single and complete surrender of our lives. There is a divine carelessness which we must acquire. We no longer preach ourselves or our accomplishments. We are not pleaders for an organization or promoters of special programs. We are witnesses for Christ, knowing at last that in him there is the light men need to live by. As we learn how to love men, we learn how to find the maximum satisfaction in our service. We may not be worldly wise, but we can be wise in knowing the secrets of God.

The man who would be the instrument in God's hands to reveal Him to men need not be the most intelligent man of his generation. He may not be the most widely traveled. Perhaps he has not been exceptionally endowed in any observable way. But he must be utterly committed to God's service and steeped in the history of the Christian movement. And he must have a burning desire to help in saving men from their blindness.

There is a poem about a poor Irish emigrant woman who found America the land of her dreams. Yet she could not forget the Irish grave where one of her children was buried and that sorrow never left her.

> I'm very happy where I am,
> Far across the say;
> I'm very happy far from home
> In North Amerikay. (But)
> A little voice still calls me back
> To my far, far counthrie,
> And nobody can hear it spake,
> Oh! Nobody but me.[7]

---

[7] Dion Boucicault in MacLean, *High Country*, 65.

And that little voice which calls men home will often call in vain. There will be many times when we alone can hear it. Then if we can interpret its meaning it may be that another lost child will return to the Father's house, or a confused soul may recover its sense of direction. It is one of the great promises given to every good minister of Jesus Christ that there will be times when he shall be to a confused generation the instrument of God's revelation.

6

The Repairer

. . . and thou shalt be called, The repairer of the breach, The restorer of paths to dwell in. ISAIAH 58:12.

THE task of making repairs is not an exciting one. It has little appeal to youth and it does not seem to fit our conception of the prophet's task. Our idea of prophetic preaching is not a patching up of the old, but a clearing of the ground for the new. We long to begin afresh and build from the ground up the society God wants. But seldom if ever does this opportunity present itself. We must begin with things as they are. We start with churches burdened with memories of the past and organizations that cannot be remade in a day. There is a vast amount of the preacher's work that is simply repair and restoration.

I have a friend who withdrew from the ministry a few years ago in order to found a Christian community in a rich agricultural valley. He had grown restless under the demands and disappointments of the church he served, and thought he might actually create a new community wherein would dwell righteousness. No one can despise that kind of spirit and that high hope. But the last time I talked with him, he seemed singularly discouraged. Things were not going too well and he had begun to doubt the possibility of carrying his plans to completion. While he did not openly confess this, I felt that he had begun to doubt the value of work that does not begin with society as it is.

Whether we like it or not, we have to repair the breach and restore the path.

So far as the scholars can tell, this part of the Book of Isaiah comes to us from a man who had returned with his people from a long exile. They had looked forward to the time when God would intervene and let them go home again, and under a liberal emperor this had happened to them. For years they had believed this event would be the end of their troubles and the beginning of their prosperity. Like many people before and after them, they had tended to exaggerate their present difficulties and grow nostalgic over the good days before their exile. Now they were face to face with the opportunity they had dreamed of for so long.

When they arrived home, they began enthusiastically to restore the land. At first their energy was unlimited and they were carried along by the joy of being home and free. They could put up with the lack of conveniences because they had been set at liberty. But it does not take too much imagination to see how this enthusiasm waned. Gradually the sheer drudgery of their task became a weight on their energy. The time arrived when weariness brought discouragement. You cannot live very long on the basis of past expectation alone.

At last, the whole project seemed to collapse. The task was so much greater than they had believed. The damage to be repaired was more than they had conceived. The future stretched out endlessly and none could see the day when the land would be reclaimed. How many long and back-breaking days of toil it would take to repair the walls alone! What a toll of energy the rebuilding of the Temple claimed! Some of them began to think of the exile as not so bad after all. Perhaps they had made too much of this independence idea. Over the people there fell a spirit of lethargy and hopelessness. They went through the motions, but life and hope were gone.

This spirit began to affect their religious life. Ritual became all important and the inner experience of faith was missing. Their social life took on the color of their pagan neighbors. Instead of being a nation redeemed by the Lord, they began to act like a tired people, still in exile. Instead of victory, they took on the color of defeat. From the heights of optimism and hope they sank into the depths of pessimism and despair. It was to such a people as this that Isaiah wrote.

Significantly, his appeal is to the religious loyalty of the people. He is at pains to restore their spiritual life and rescue them from their lifeless worship. He knows that unless their faith is restored and their loyalty to God safeguarded, nothing can go right with them, so he speaks to their spiritual natures and he makes great promises in the name of God. They must recapture the living experience of fellowship with God. Then they shall be able to repair the breach and restore the paths. But the problem, as always, is a spiritual one; for until God builds the city or the nation, the builders do their work in vain.

Now there is a sense in which this present situation is very similar to the one we have just described. We, too, have been in exile, though not under the control of a foreign power. But we have been exiled by war. Everything was different during that period and many of the familiar experiences had to be discontinued. Young men left their homes and circled the earth; people were uprooted and moved into new environments. There was a kind of rootlessness in living which affected our spirits. We knew fear and concern for sons and daughters. With great longing we remembered our life before the exile of war and we dreamed of the day when we might return home. This was all we asked and it seemed to us that it would be the answer to all our problems. Once we could recover the freedom and safety of that earlier time, all would be well. In spite of the warnings of some gloomy prophets, we could not believe that the postwar problems could equal the postwar satisfactions.

Now we are not so sure. It is not as good as we thought it would be. We are not back to the good days we remembered, or perhaps we had idealized them too much. After the first burst of enthusiasm, we began to slow down the rebuilding processes. We had promised ourselves that this time we would build a world that was war-proof, but we started the same equivocation, the same lying, the same selfishness, almost before the last gun sounded. None of us is willing to give up very much, and soon the old suspicions begin to raise their heads. Our chief ally has become our worst enemy and men begin to say—at first timidly but now openly—that the next war has to be planned for and we know who our enemy will be. In fits of despondency and fear the people have surrendered their liberties and gone on witch hunts.

But the real danger is the lack of faith in God and in ourselves. Our religion has taken on a mummified appearance. We keep it for exhibition purposes but we do not live by it. The appalling thing is the insecurity of our people. We begin to act like a defeated nation instead of a victorious one, as we make mountains out of molehills and see communists under every bed. We are the perfect example of a nation with tremendous resources and no faith.

It is not too much to say that Isaiah's situation was greatly similar to the minister's situation today. His word is ours, and we must become repairers of the breach in the wall, and restorers of the paths. It is our task to keep the courage of men strong and prevent the flood of fear and barbarism from overwhelming us. We, too, live in the midst of an emergency.

I. The Breach in the Wall

There are a number of people who profess to see nothing extraordinary in the present crisis. This is simply the postwar ennui, they will tell us, and it is not more serious than other similar periods after other wars. They still cling to the hope that the problems can be solved by force or the threat of force. They think that if we keep armed and prevent the economic system from collapsing, all may yet be well. At least, they insist, we can win the next war. Every now and again some prominent man gains attention by proclaiming in oracular tone that all is well with us. To the religious man this has a hollow sound because such a man has no concept of spiritual realities. For it is apparent that the breach is not a thing of armaments, but of spirit.

The idea of a breach is a familiar one to Christians because they begin with the understanding that there is a breach in human life. However we may interpret the Atonement, Christians have never doubted that it is God's act to heal the breach which sin had caused between our lives and His. Paul's description of the gap between desire and fulfillment on the part of the natural man is the truth about human nature. We do not like to speak of ourselves today as "fallen creatures," but whether we like it or not, it describes the condition of men until they have been redeemed by God.

This should be easy for even modern skeptics to accept, for it is the testimony of psychoanalysis. Once we get down deep into the hearts of modern men, we find there is a breach in their nature and they are split creatures. As a matter of fact, there is not just one breach, but many. The attainment of wholeness is the aim of the psychologist as well as the minister, and they both agree that there is a schism of the soul and a terrible division in the heart. The healing of this condition was supposed to be possible by knowledge. Some have tried to heal it by removing the sense of guilt. Others have allowed men to push responsibility on them and have become permanent leaning posts for troubled spirits.

For the Christian, of course, the healing is in Christ. He came to bridge the gap between men and God, between men and men, between a man and his true self. We have been through a period when ministers have tried to heal the people lightly by means of a shallow liberalism. We must return to the orthodox Christian view that men are healed only by the act of God in Christ. We may begin, therefore, with the assumption that there is a breach in life which can be healed only by faith.

But there is also a breach in our common life because we have quite misunderstood the nature of civilization. It has seemed to us a result of automatic processes which once started went on without much conscious thought or effort. It was assumed that, once men began to live together in societies, the external conditions would determine the nature of their lives and the qualities of their communities. Climate, for example, was one of the main factors. But the significance of deliberate effort and free choice was played down until it was practically negligible. It is hard for us to realize how far in the direction of dialectical materialism we had gone, until the Communists came along and made that theory unpatriotic.

I venture to say that we have missed essential clues in coming to a true understanding of civilization. The building of civilized life is more like the building of dykes around a little island to keep out the sea of barbarism. There is never a safe time when men can relax and assume that the danger is over. For there are forces within every group—indeed, within our own hearts—that will weaken the banks whenever there is an opportunity. If we might change the figure for a moment, civilization is like a man sitting by the fire in the midst of the jungle. Around him, peering hungrily, are the beasts of prey who wait for their chance to spring. Let the man drowse or get careless and they are on him. The price of civilization, like the price of liberty, is eternal vigilance.

Today we have a good illustration of how civilization is lost. A few years ago, Germany was regarded by many as the most civilized nation in the world. At least, in the pursuits which we associate with high culture, she excelled. German music was at the top; German science was respected everywhere; German literature could hold its own in any competition. It is hard for us to realize that even in the theological realm Germany was considered supreme. When a young man wanted to teach in an American theological seminary, a Ph.D. from a German school of theology was a real advantage. So much of the leading work on the Old and New Testaments was done by German scholars. In any theological discussion more than one German theologian was almost certain to be quoted. There was a graciousness of life, a romantic atmosphere, that created for Germany not only respect but affection. Let us never forget the picture of this Germany, if for no other reason than to warn us of the danger all people are in at all times.

For, almost overnight, historically speaking, all of this changed. The man drowsed by the fire and the beasts were on him. The wild, untamed spirits were let loose to breach the dykes. The siren singers of revenge were listened to, and behold, it was a pleasant melody they sang. Then before most people knew what had happened or how it had happened, the Nazis were in control and the nation was on its terrible way to death. We have seen evil unexcelled, even by savage tribes. We have watched a people drop from the heights of civilization to the depths of savagery, and from the best to the worst, in a brief moment of time, has been the story of Germany. But the most terrible thing about the story is the obvious fact that the evil was not contained in one culture nor was it the possession of one nation. Else why was the rest of the world so long in recognizing Hitler for what he was? Why did many another national leader look upon him with ill-concealed admiration? And why has the destruction of Germany and the death of Hitler given us no consolation? Because Germany is a symbol, but not the whole evil thing in itself. Every nation's life stands under the constant threat of traitors waiting for a chance to breach the barriers and let in the powers of tyranny and torture.

Today we have a new feeling about this civilization of ours. It is not as eternal and secure as we thought. We can no longer assume that the victory has been achieved finally. Unless we are willing to be heroic in our defense, there is no guarantee that our children shall have our achievements to enjoy. Sensitive writers have been aware of this beating surge of savagery for some time. H. G. Wells wrote about it in several of his books and finally confessed his fear that mind had come to the end of its tether. Nietzsche's awful prophecy does not not seem so impossible now:

Is it not inevitable that men will finally renounce all that is comforting, holy and healing, all hope and all faith in the hidden harmony of the world, in future bliss and justification? Is it not inevitable that men should renounce God and that, out of cruelty towards themselves, they should worship the stone, that which is stupid and heavy, fate, nothingness? To sacrifice God for nothingness—this paradoxical cruelty has been kept in reserve for the generation about to rise; we all know something about it.[1]

When the war broke out in Europe, the Nazis occupied the Dutch Island of Walcheren. When the British decided they must be removed, they joined forces with the ancient enemy of the Island, the sea, and bombed the dykes, flooding the land. But many of the stubborn Dutch people stayed on. Forty thousand remained, while gradually the thirty thousand which had been evacuated returned. They timed their work so they could arrive home again before the high tide rolled down the streets and into the country roads. They lived in the tops of the houses for everything else was under water. You will remember that during this time there was considerable complaining in our country because gasoline was rationed and we had to curb our pleasure driving.

Here is a parable! The sea has been let in on our land. The dykes have been breached. We wade through the hatred, the cruelty, the black hopelessness of barbarism. For a long time in the future this will be our fate. In the meantime, we must repair

[1] Quoted in *Man's Disorder and God's Design,* II, 50.

the dykes and restore the paths. It is a time which demands a stubbornness on our part and a heroism beyond our usual practice. Those who lust for the easy days of the past and the comfortable living of established society will fail in this crisis. Not in many a year has the threat been so real and so final.

II. Nature of the Breach

Now we must make sure that we understand the nature of this break. The reason so many well-meaning people are of little help in this crucial time is that they have no idea of what has happened. To them, we are in the midst of a passing crisis in economics which will be settled before too long by some new inventions or some new gadgets. Or they assume that our troubles are political or military in essence. But until we see that this is something of the spirit, we are unprepared for the testing ahead, and this is what makes the situation so serious. For it is precisely the spiritual problem which is the most difficult to grasp and solve. We are clever people when it is only a matter of dealing with the material difficulties, and in that realm we do the impossible and accomplish the miraculous. But when we face spiritual emptiness, we are over our heads. The first task of the minister is to make clear to the people what the break is and what the crisis means.

For one thing, it is a return to naturalism which has breached our dykes. There was a song on Broadway some time ago which described the joys of "doing what comes naturally." This spirit assumes that we get along best when we do not take duty seriously nor strive to be something higher than the beast. We are simply animals who have learned to talk, according to this point of view, and if we live in harmony with that concept, we shall have a good time without all the pain which comes to men who strive for something more. This view is a denial of the reality of man's spiritual longings. It will not believe that the hunger of the soul is an essential hunger.

Back of this acceptance of naturalism, there is the selfish desire to do as we please. We have been prepared for this attitude by all the nonsense taught us about repressions. One would think, if he followed the pseudopsychological jargon of the day, the most harmful thing a man can do is not to obey every impulse. If we are to be healthy, we have been told, we must do whatever we desire to do. People even raise their children on that basis. But after we have followed merrily along this path for any distance, it comes to us suddenly one day that life has lost its significance. On this road lies madness, for the undisciplined life is the meaningless life. It was the path taken by the "lost generation" after World War I. It is the path taken by every man who is no longer willing to assume his share of the responsibility for keeping life decent, and it comes home to us at last that it is not the Galilean, but Naturalism, whose breath turns the world gray.

The break is an ethical one. It has been a denial of right and wrong and a refusal to accept moral distinctions. Again we have the glaring example in the Nazis, but let us not be so foolish as to assume it was limited to them. Everything is to be condoned if it wins, is a general maxim. There is to be no relationship recognized between means and ends. If we succeed, all will be forgiven, and if we fail, nothing will matter anyway. That has been the slimy thing which has come through the breach from the sea of barbarism.

A few years ago we would not have believed it possible that men should insist seriously that lying is right. We were not so good that we never lied and pretended it was truth, but we never took the position that you could make a virtue out of lying. We have done just that in these days. Propaganda which assumes the right to lie and extols the virtue of telling the same lie until it is believed, becomes more prevalent and less shocking. Under the threat of outside danger, we are quite willing to dispense with the truth and justify our act as a national virtue. The vice which seemed so reprehensible when it was far off in the land of the enemy, loses its repugnance when there is a profit to be gained by practicing it at home. When one surveys the postwar scene, one wonders who won the real victory. We can hardly escape the conclusion that Hitler, being dead, yet lives.

We were never so naïve as to believe that hatred did not exist, but up to now most of us paid lip service to the idea of love. Rapidly we seem to be moving toward the line where it is to be regarded as a crime to love the enemy, or even suggest that we try another method than force. Can it be true that we are approaching the place where a man shall be accused of un-Americanism because he is loyal to the law of love? Is the flood running too high for us to stop it? Are we to continue under the domination of the philosophy justified during the war, that we must make hate our ruling passion?

Perhaps the most serious part of this ethical break is the assumption that no evil will result from hating or lying. There seems to be a loss of the sense of moral law and moral reality. We are encouraged to believe that hatred will pay a big dividend and lying will bring us no bad results. It seems to be true that a vast number of people are caught in the flood of doubt concerning retribution for the practice of immorality. We think we can use the sword and not fall by it. We have drugged ourselves into believing that God does not make the same demands on us He makes on our opponents. We begin to talk blithely about our use of a hydrogen bomb in the next war, though it was only a short time ago that we agreed an atomic bomb must never be used again. And we were outraged that any nation should believe for one minute that we could not be trusted with it.

The breach is a return to nihilism. Words seem to mean nothing. Perhaps the most serious defeat that has come to us out of the war has been the loss of certain great words upon which we have built our Western world. What does truth mean any more? It is a term to confuse our enemies and to be used as a means to some selfish end. It is a term of convenience but no longer one of universal application. Or what does mercy mean when used by a Communist? He has told us already that everything is to be justified which helps the party and no man has a right to stand in the way of the party. Will mercy have any general meaning to him? None whatever, for he will gladly accept it for himself but he will deny it to his enemies. Does he feel any compulsion to be merciful to all men at all times? Apparently not!

With the ceaseless, monotonous chattering of the radio which invades a man's privacy wherever he goes and however he travels, we have become killers of words. Does "the best" mean anything except something somebody wants to sell? No wonder we become an unbelieving people. We have no real verbal currency. We have devaluated our vocabularies until we have no way of stating important, eternal verities. We listen but we do not believe. We have ears to hear but we hear not. The flood of noise over the air is a part of the flood which threatens to drown our way of life.

George Thomas, the son of a London dustman, was the victim of a progressive muscular atrophy which gave him little to look forward to but a constant worsening of his physical condition. Yet, through self-education, he learned about many things and developed an interest in life. He wrote a book entitled: *My Mind a Kingdom*. He made this significant confession:

I have not found life a great adventure, but mostly an unbearable trial, and the only thing I know for certain is that I have to go on. I have often thought of giving up the struggle, but as long as I can do anything at all I must do it. And so it comes about that I enjoy most things, even the fight.

The Christian minister today will find himself in a similar situation. The struggle is not going to be easy. But we know one thing—we must do our job—we must go on. Because we know the seriousness of the situation, it will give us joy to be a part of the fight. For the breach is a spiritual one, and we hold our commissions from God to be "repairers of the breach."

III. How Shall the Breach be Repaired?

Having seen the nature of the breach, it becomes apparent at once that much of our effort to better our present situation is in vain. As long as we are dealing with something that is spiritual in nature, it is foolishness to use force in our treatment. That only makes it worse. The spiritual breach will be healed only by spiritual power. Thus every increase in military might and every attempt to give us security through physical means defeats itself. Instead of healing the breach, these methods widen it. Whether we think these methods are justified or not, it ought to be plain to any man that they do not go to the heart of the trouble, and they have no promise in them.

We must create faith again. The world is full of empty lives which are incapable of constructive action. Think of the young German who grew up between the wars without hope in the future. Watch him give himself to the totalitarian philosophy in a desperate hope that this is at least something to give life purpose. See him after the debacle of the defeat, and think of him now without faith in God or men. Can we expect to build much of a world on the basis of his emptiness? Multiply him by thousands and we begin to see the real problem our world is facing.

Somehow this man has to believe that life makes sense. Once again he has to have faith in some value that will enable him to sacrifice for remote and mighty ends. In a word, he has to find God and believe that there is something eternal upon which a man may venture his whole life. We are not the kind of creatures who can exist in a vacuum. We have to feel that there is One who makes the business of living significant. We can exist without prosperity and without comfort, but we cannot live without faith in God. If the devil of Nazism has been expelled, seven more devils will return to the empty lives of an empty culture.

The present crisis is a spiritual one. It is useless to talk about reeducation in democracy by a people who have lost their faith in the foundation of democracy. The one thing that would give men faith again would be a great religious revival of profound intensity. This, of course, is something for the churches to consider. It is also something that every minister must face, because it is his responsibility. It is for us to live in such loving proximity with the Galilean that our faith may become compelling and powerful again.

We must bring hope back into the world. The Church stands today like Elijah after his victory over the priests of Baal. In the nervous depression which followed, when a wicked queen sought his life, he fled to the desert and sulked. His complaint was that he alone was left among the faithful and he had proved no better than his fathers. Then God gave him food and sent him to the mountain of Horeb where he dwelt in a cave. After the wind had passed, and the earthquake shock was over, and the fire had raged, he heard the still, small voice. He was given marching orders again with the proclamation: "Yet I have left me seven thousand in Israel, all the knees which have not bowed unto Baal, and every mouth hath not kissed him" (I Kings 19:18). So we ought to be aware of the resources which are the Church's in this dark time. We are a world-wide fellowship with enough potential power to change the world overnight. We have committed to us the most compelling story the world has ever known and the most powerful Gospel men have ever heard. We can count on the response of the human heart to the good news. We follow a Christ who is always breaking out with some new impulse and creating some marvelous vision. There is less reason for Christians to be feeling sorry for themselves than there was for Elijah.

Many of us have had the privilege during the past few years of sending packages of food and clothing abroad. Some of us have sent gifts to families we did not know. I cannot forget a letter which came from a man I have never seen. He said, "Your package arrived at just the right time. But in spite of our physical needs which you supplied, you did even more. You rekindled hope in our hearts. We said that if an unknown Christian friend in America cared enough for us to send us food, we could believe in men and God." No people have been given the opportunity of repairing the breach as have we Americans. To paraphrase a word of Churchill: Never before could so few restore hope to so many. And when it comes to repairing the breach, every action of decency which conquers bitterness and lifts up a heart is worth tenfold the building of another gun.

We must bring love back into human relations. You cannot build an iron curtain that will keep love out and you cannot wall the minds of men against its entrance. We must bring it back into our personal relations and believe that one deed done in love is worth a million vague speeches on keeping America strong. Here is the universal language which in a day of conflicting ideologies is the only way we can communicate with one another. There was an employer who startled applicants for jobs by breaking in, apropos to nothing, with this question: "By the way, would you like to build a bridge?" If the man in sudden surprise would reply, "What? Me? Why, yes, as a matter of fact I would like to build a bridge," he was hired on the spot. For the man who wanted to bring together two separated places was sure to have imagination and constructive ideas. So it is that our Lord comes to us with that same question: "Would you like to build a bridge across the chasms separating mankind? Would you like to unite a divided world?" And if we answer in the affirmative, then we are called at once into close fellowship with him in this mighty task of healing the breach and building the new community.

IV. WHO SHALL REPAIR THE BREACH?

Albert Jay Nock has a piece called *Isaiah's Job*. In it, God sends the prophet to tell the people what a worthless lot they are and warn them of a coming destruction. But the prophet is told also that his warning will not do any noticeable good and he will be fortunate to get out with his life. Isaiah raises the obvious question: What is the use of going if the result is to be failure? Then God replies that there is a remnant—an inarticulate minority who will return and build the new society. The future depends upon them and it is the prophet's job to be their voice and their shepherd.

We need that word for ourselves. In our time there is a remnant without voice or champion. The Christian ministry is sent to them. They will return, and they will build. God never leaves any generation without that saving remnant. They represent His creative minority and their work is the hope of tomorrow. They are stubborn and courageous because they know God and believe that the future belongs to Him. They are never a majority at any time, but like the leaven, they exert a pervading influence in all of society.

There is a fine passage in a postwar book:

In Holland alone a passion for conquest still smolders and grows with the centuries: to create land out of water—not only to defend, but to assault and push back; to paint green, bit by bit, what is blue on the map. To grow grain where fish have swum; to ride horses where the monotonous waves have marched; in most Hollanders this passion remains unconscious.[2]

Something of that is the spirit of the saving remnant. In them there is the passion to sow love where hatred rolls, to drive back barbarism and increase the area of civilization. When the dykes have been breached, they wait until once again they may begin their assault on the sea. They are the ones who always repair the breaks in the wall. Usually they are Christians, or at least deeply influenced by Christ.

The early Christians did this in the early centuries of this era. It was the City of God which remained after the City of Rome

[2] Doolard, *Roll Back the Sea,* Simon and Schuster, 1948.

had been sacked. The early Methodists did it in eighteenth-century England. If we have any doubts about our ability to repair the breach in this day, they should be expelled when we realize that our fathers have done it in other difficult times. If this is a terrifying responsibility, it is also an ennobling one. We must stop hoping that somehow things will just work out. We must have no confidence in the way of conquest and the threat of military destruction. We must bring to bear all the spiritual resources we have and begin the slow and painful task of driving back the sea and rebuilding the dykes.

A coast guard crew had received a signal of distress and prepared to launch the boat, though the sea was still high and the boat was small. A spectator criticized the captain for attempting to reach the ship and endangering the lives of the whole crew. He said, "You don't expect to come back, do you?" The captain replied, "Don't know nothin' about comin' back. The regulations say you have to go out—but nothin' about comin' back." The time has come when we ministers have to take that same uncompromising stand. Our way is not easy and we shall be subject to attack on every hand, but we have to repair the breach in the face of many dangers. Our confidence is in the word of our Lord: "For whosoever will save his life shall lose it: but whosoever shall lose his life for my sake and the gospel's, the same shall save it" (Mark 8:35). And it is this spirit which can make us the "repairers of the breach."

7

The Saint

To all that be in Rome, beloved of God, called to be saints. . . .
ROMANS 1:7

W E HAVE tended to equate sainthood with stuffiness, and few
modern persons get much thrill out of contemplating such
a status. We shy away from the idea as if it were something
disgraceful. If the younger generation felt that being religious
meant being saints, they would flee from it even more than they
do. We reserve the term for the dead or for the rare individual
like Gandhi, who never seemed to quite belong to this age.

There are some students who study the life of the mystics in
order to penetrate into the mysteries of religious experience.
The lives of the saints are objects of psychological analysis, but
seldom of emulation. We often make prayer the subject of study,
and there are experts in the field who can tell all about the way
it works and why it seems to work, though they never pray. To
modern man there seems to be something quaint about the whole
concept of the consecrated devotional life.

This reflects the departmentalizing of our life. If religion is
not a way of life but one interest among many, then the serious
practice of it is only a special career to be chosen by a few
strange, not entirely normal, people. We have the unexpressed
idea that to be a saint is to take up a particular profession as a

118

man might go in for any special career. We read in the paper
that a successful businessman and his wife decide to leave their
home and give up the world for the monastery and the nunnery.
They speak about the whole matter as if it were a choice that
one has to make in terms of one's whole work. Apparently they
assumed that the normal lives of a married couple in the business
world could not have been completely religious. We think of
what they have given up and we regard them as peculiar. But
we are more certain than ever before that this religious business,
when carried too far, does strange things to people and it is best
not to give it too much attention. The emphasis on separate
orders, and the insistence that to be most pleasing to God one
must withdraw from the world, fits in with our secular views
of religious living.

As Christians, we must re-examine this whole matter and
rethink our whole viewpoint. There are a few who assume that
the redemption of our society is impossible. Like the apocalyptists in other crucial times, they feel that society will continue to
get worse until God acts from the outside. This action will be
in the nature of a catastrophe which will bring history to an end
and begin the new age. Whatever the end of the world means
to men, it often carries with it a hopelessness concerning the
present age. We must confess that there is much in contemporary
life to give comfort to the champions of this view. Things do
seem to be out of hand, and as far ahead as we can see, there is
no great change to be expected. The worst thing about these
people is their ill-concealed satisfaction as they describe the
coming end, usually in terms of the flaming metaphors of
Daniel or Revelation.

But if this is not to be the end of the process, then we must
believe that the life of men can be redeemed from within. If
God is not going to act in terms of catastrophe and sudden death,
then He will act in terms of released spiritual power through
individuals. If the reform is not to come through external inter-

vention, then it must be attained through character. We are forced to make a decision in this matter. The apocalyptist can find a melancholy joy in the very momentum which carries us farther toward judgment, because this means that God's intervention is so much nearer. But if we are to assume that God will redeem the world through men, then we are driven to accept our responsibility to be instruments for the working of the redeeming act. We are, in a word, called to be saints, if we are not satisfied to be mere describers of the future destruction.

The proclamation of the Gospel is always a judgment on the world. It speaks a cutting word concerning the pride, the immorality, the materialism of any age. But unless it is more than that, it fails to change life or give hope for tomorrow. It has to provide a demonstration of the New Life. It has to illustrate the answer in action. This is the reason the Church is an essential part of the Christian witness. We can have no Christianity without the Church, because we must have a demonstration, even if incomplete and imperfect, of what the Gospel wills to do. Paul understood this so clearly that he emphasized the fellowship even when he believed that the end was near. The people of those early churches were "called to be saints," which is to say they were to show what life in Christ meant in the society of that day. So it is that when the Church makes wealth or political power a substitute for the demonstration of this New Life, it fails. In one of the most bitter attacks in all literature, Dostoevski insisted that atheism was the child of the Roman Church because that Church had become simply a continuation of the Roman Empire. In this distortion of what the Church ought to be, the Russian writer regarded it as the Antichrist. When one studies his words carefully, he seems to be saying that the creation of saints is the purpose of the Christian fellowship, and the denial of that purpose throws the Church on the side of the enemies of Christ.

We would do well to think of that word in our time. It has an application not only to Roman Catholicism but to all highly organized, wealthy, powerful, religious institutions. It is so easy for us to become a part of the opposition while still swearing allegiance to our Lord. For when the chief aim of the fellowship is not to create saints—not to demonstrate what life with Christ means—then we have missed the goal. There was something of this high understanding of our real purpose in the early Methodist class meetings. The meeting was not primarily for social purposes but for spiritual searchings. Questions were asked about the inner life and probings were made into the spiritual health of individual Christians. It was the genius of John Wesley to devise methods for sharing inspiration with other Christians by keeping men aware of the primary aim of the fellowship. Such procedure can turn into morbid self-examination, or it can become shallow and exhibitionistic in its spirit. But the modern church has gone too far away from the obligation to provide opportunities for people to help one another become saints. Certainly this is one appeal of the sects. They have more of the sense of being a people called to demonstrate the grace of God in the common life.

The man in the street has a sense of disappointment with the Church. He does not know how to phrase it and he may never have thought it through to conscious definition. He drifts along on the outside, but there may have been times when he tried to get interested in what religion is all about. He has the feeling, however, that if there is nothing in the Church but what can be found in the club or the lodge, then the Church has betrayed him. He is looking for the marks of holiness on the church members. He has the unmistakable feeling that if Christianity is what the preachers keep telling him it is, then it ought to make a difference in the lives of those who profess to be the products of it. Holiness is vitally attractive and its absence from the life of the Church leaves a great emptiness which nothing else can fill. Like any other way of life, Christianity has to produce or die.

We must turn, therefore, to a consideration of the Christian saint and his challenge to us. We must face the inescapable implication in the Christian teaching that Christ transforms the lives of men. We have to believe that we ourselves, as ministers, are first of all called to embark on the adventure of becoming demonstrations of sainthood. Then we must have the courage to call our people to their saintly callings.

I. Toward a Definition

There are some people who make sainthood a matter of correct doctrine. Thus the gentle, Christlike soul who differs from them theologically would never be accepted by these people as a saint. But some cantankerous, hard-minded person, who clings tenaciously to the right doctrine, would be welcomed into the fellowship. There is often an unlikable quality in the lives of men who hold an unwavering loyalty to what they conceive to be the true doctrine. Perhaps it is contact with such "saints" that makes the following lines so easy to understand:

> To live with the saints in Heaven
> Is bliss and glory;
> To live with the saints on earth
> Is—often another story.[1]

When we are speaking of saints, we are talking more of a quality of the heart than a quality of the mind. For unlovely lives can believe intellectually in good things. Jesus was always sympathetic to people who got into trouble through their emotions, but he had very hard things to say about men whose evil was a product of the hardened heart and the unloving spirit. For Christianity, the main thing is love. With our modern insistence that respectability is the sign of religion, we miss the point concerning the saints. They may not be accepted in the best circles, and they are not always the men who have gotten on in the

[1] *Atlantic Monthly*, October, 1928.

world. But the one quality which they never lack is the loving heart.

Nor should we expect perfection of disposition at all times. I have no doubt but that the Apostle Paul was often hard to live with and not always amiable. But he had the gift of quick repentance and he could make a swift apology. He might lose his patience in the white heat of his enthusiasm, but he would never be deliberately mean. We are not speaking of a passive gentleness at all times, for the saints were fighters and tenacious in their loyalty. We are impressed, however, with the lack of cold, calculated selfishness on their part, and we are drawn to their warm and open affections.

The saint has a childlike lack of self-consciousness. He would be the last man even to hint that he should be called a saint. It is never a matter of achieving some static perfectionism, and indeed, one of the most terrible sights in the world is to look on a man who has concluded he has a mission to reform mankind. Such a man may accomplish some good and be of some value to society, but he will never be a saint. A man must be himself, and have the elemental simplicity of the unsophisticated. In any art there is no real achievement until the artist has given up all effort to fit any preconceived pattern. In art it is sure death to accept an artificial role or play a false part. Living is an art and the man who most succeeds in being real has the best chance of becoming a saint.

We talk much about equality and sometimes assume it to be the fundamental Christian virtue. It is a fundamental democratic necessity, but there is a sense in which it is not a Christian virtue at all. Men must be treated equally, but they do not have equal gifts nor are they of equal virtue. Each man has his own part to play and he must be himself with all his differences. He must not be ashamed of his uniqueness, and the saint is aware of this truth for himself. He is a part of the fellowship, but his part is no mere copy of any other man's part. The unity of the Christian society is a unity of difference. That is why the saint always seems to be over and above the crowd, and yet he never withdraws himself from his brethren. He knows how to be in the world, but not of the world.

Nor should we assume that once the holy state has been achieved the quest is over and the questions answered finally. Father George Tyrrell came as close to this state as possible and he represents the Catholic ideal:

In all my life, now fully forty-seven years, I cannot remember a single temptation against faith that seemed to me to have any force. The church's teaching is before me, as a glorious series of splendid certainties. My mind is absolutely satisfied, . . . I have no private judgment to overcome, and no desire to exercise my private judgment. It is a greater pleasure to receive and possess truth with certainty, than to go in search of it and be in uncertainty whether it has been found.[2]

One reads such a statement and gasps. Can the man have truly understood himself? Has he not misread the past experience of his life? Or does the Roman Catholic Church have the power to create this kind of assurance? We know that it does not work for all men because they have confessed to a greatly different experience. But for Protestants, such a state is not only impossible, but it is undesirable. It certainly was not the experience of the writers of the Psalms. It was not even true of Jesus. Saints are always at ease, but they are not necessarily at rest.

The saint seems to be a man who is going in one direction with all his might. He has achieved single-mindedness. His devotion to his Lord is complete and he knows the perfection of love. There may be times when the question rises and the doubt assails. He is not always certain of the next step and he must often quench the rebel sigh. But he has settled one thing once and for all—he is going to live in the spirit of his Lord as he

[2] Quoted by Phillips, *op. cit.,* 87.

understands him. Having taken that one vital step, he knows peace of mind and power of purpose. He has learned how to love men because he loves God. The mystic is not necessarily a saint, for the mystical experience is not necessarily incompatible with egotism. The knowledge of a superior experience can easily result in spiritual pride, and this is especially true if a man stays only within the general propositions of our faith. Our defense and safety lie in practicing the love of God in specific places and in relation to individual men.

The attitude of the saint toward other men is one of the sure signs by which he may be recognized. For the joy of sanctity is manifest in his purified vision of his brethren. Saints see their fellows through the eyes of God and they come close to having the second sight which observes motives and penetrates into the heart. For our own guidance, we can be sure we are moving in the right direction if we find it easier to put up with unlovely people and find sympathy for obstreperous men with whom God has decreed we must work. It is possible to help the saintly process along by never putting into words our impatience and our dislike. Once we have given dislike the reality of expression, we have made it doubly hard to overcome it. We ought not to say it, but wait patiently for some hidden ray to shine forth from the dark places of our irritation. We are achieving spiritual maturity when we begin to see the virtues in men which are hidden by their imperfections.

Objectivity is one of the saint's qualities. He does not wallow around in his own emotions and get lost in his own feelings. He never makes the inner experience an end in itself. This is the pathway to failure, for we are then in great danger of mistaking the feeling of interior glow for the sign of infallibility. Men become dangerous when their religion is only subjective experience. This is one of the main reasons the saints of the Bible were not solitary but a part of the community.

The New Testament does not talk about "the saint," it talks

about "the saints." The use of the plural is most significant and we should be careful to observe its implications. Saints seem to need one another for encouragement and for criticism. They seem to need the opportunity of service. They do not reflect the hothouse sensitivity of some modern would-be perfectionists who cannot bear the rough jostling of the crowd. They have the power to live with people and yet be citizens of heaven. Blake's wife, who lived with him for forty-five understanding years, once remarked:

Mr. Blake has been so little with me. For though in body we never were separated, he was incessantly away in Paradise.[3]

To live in the world and serve its needs, yet to have "one foot in heaven," is the gift of these spiritual leaders.

Baron von Hügel said that there were four conditions which a man must fulfill before he is recognized as a saint by the Roman Catholic Church. First, he must have been loyal to the Church. Second, he must have been heroic. Third, he must have had spiritual power beyond ordinary human capacity. Fourth, he must have had a radiant spirit through all the experiences of his life. There is implied in these qualities one which underlies them all and interpenetrates them all: ". . . if therefore thine eye be single, thy whole body shall be full of light" (Matthew 6:22).

II. SIGNIFICANCE OF BEING

It is our belief that the word "do" is much to be preferred over the word "believe." We like "action" better than "faith." We have gone all out for activity and we have minimized the quality of a man's character. This is the main reason we think very little about saints except as curiosities or as a strange people who are dead. What we think or what we are has not seemed very

[3] Quoted by Nelson, *Our Roving Bible,* Abingdon-Cokesbury, 1945, 140.

important; it is only important to act, says the modern creed. The blundering man who does the wrong thing but does it loudly has been more admired than the man who is not sure that action wrongly directed is of any particular help. The harm we have done by acting from wrong motives and immature purposes can hardly be overestimated, and there is a great need to find the balance between action and being.

One of the most impressive things about spiritual men is their ability to wait. Those who see action as an end in itself must forever plunge ahead on some track or other. They have no time to get their directions or to pause for a view of the situation. The long years of waiting and preparation in the life of Jesus, or Paul's sojourn in the desert, would be impossible for the hurried men who must grasp their reward now. The patient plodding of Gandhi was totally misunderstood by the Nazis, and it is unappreciated by us, for that matter. Yet it would seem not beyond the realm of possibility that the Indian Saint may yet win a victory which was denied the men forever in a hurry. Just from the standpoint of efficiency, which is one of our gods, we had better give more consideration to the condition of our inner life.

It is the men with inner qualities who represent the future's hope. As H. G. Wells once said:

I am building my expectation of a new phase of human affairs upon the belief that there is a profoundly serious minority in the mass of our generally indifferent species. I cannot understand the existence of any of the great religions. I cannot explain any fine and grave constructive process in history, unless there is such a serious minority amidst our confusions. They are the Salt of the Earth, these people capable of devotion and of living lives for remote and mighty ends.[4]

He was describing the saints.

It is remarkable how little lasting impression the activists may make on history when we compare them with the men who stress

[4] Quoted by Toynbee, *A Study of History*, III, Oxford, 1935, 239.

being. Action is all very well, but it must be directed toward right goals and have a spiritual quality within it. Men who give their lives to doing, without consideration of their aims, are not the possessors of the future. It is amazing how quickly they are forgotten and how unforgettable are the neglected men who established some new advance in the realm of the spirit. There seems to be something in the Universe which is not impressed with directionless movement. Long after the world has forgotten the headline makers of one generation, it remembers the quiet men whose spiritual contributions enriched their own time and the future.

Perhaps the greatest departure from Jesus that modern Christians have taken is their refusal to believe that the quality of a man's life is the ultimate thing. This is the reason we are so out of sympathy with his judgments of sin. What he thought was serious, we take as unimportant; but what he considered forgivable, we find difficult to condone. He was always looking into the heart and trying to diagnose the motive. We are not too concerned with that, but stress the outward behavior and appearance. Many a Christian in our time, who feels himself one of the chosen few, would have been rejected by Jesus because of his willingness to substitute respectability for spiritual poverty. When we understand our Lord's reversal of the judgments of his own day, we shall see him reversing the common judgments of ours.

The New Testament assumed that the good man will produce good actions. The Pauline stress on salvation by faith was a part of this same basic understanding. It was not that man is saved by the right creed, but that a man is saved when his heart is right and his motives are in harmony with the will of God. This was the chief criticism which Jesus made against the Pharisees. They had finally arrived at a place where right actions were the ultimate test and the condition of the man's heart was of secondary importance. I do not see how we can escape the conclusion that Jesus was suspicious of pious actions when the motive was uncertain. But he found it easy to forgive the man who made mistakes if his heart was clean and his attitude toward his fellows brotherly.

Our tendency is to follow the Pharisees rather than Jesus. We are not too concerned with the spirit but we are strict in our judgment of the deed. We have said openly that what a man does is all that counts, as if you could ignore his reasons for action and the spirit of his life. We have said that to do good is fundamental, for that will automatically mean that a man is good. So we have had our ostentatious givers and our tainted funds for service institutions. We have forgiven the paganism by which the fortune was attained, if the man did a "good" deed, which was often the giving of a gift out of great abundance and, incidentally, the reducing of his income tax.

Is it not true that in the average church the saint does not fare too well? At least he seldom receives the place higher up but is merely tolerated as one of the members who cannot contribute very much to the budget. The men who take authority in the Church are the men of affairs with executive ability. They are the men of influence—"the men of distinction." But the humble spirit among us, who is goodness personified, is often an embarrassment to the Church. His ways are not our ways.

We are in need of a complete rethinking of the place of being in our scale of values. Perhaps the reason our society is not more kind and better equipped spiritually is our failure to keep first things first. Perhaps the greatest witness the Church can make in our time is to get back to the emphasis Jesus placed on the quality of the inner life. It could be that we are not going to change the world through programs and organized movements. At long last we may have to go back to the way of personal goodness—the way of the saint.

L. J. Sharp once gave this description of a certain minister's preaching:

My dear friends, you must repent—*as it were;* and be converted—*in a measure;* or you will be damned—*to a certain extent.*[5]

Something of that same lack of sharpness is discernible in our consideration of Christian character. We can forgive so much in the case of the man who has. We have so little relative enthusiasm for the man who is. The minister, especially, needs to hear again Paul's admonitions to those "called to be saints."

III. GOD'S WITNESS

The power of the Christian saint has been minimized because our thinking is colored by mass movements and power combinations. What can one man do? is a constant cry among us. Even the ministry has put more stress on executive ability than it has on sainthood. Forsyth's admonition to theological students is not amiss for us:

Gentlemen, you are not here to graduate in the University of London. You may or may not do that. You are here to graduate in Christ and His ministry.[6]

It is this quality which is the unique thing possessed by the ministry. All of its other activities are but copies of what goes on in the commercial world, just as the organization of the medieval Church was a replica of the form of the Roman Empire. If we are to make any unique contribution to the world, it will have to be as graduates of Christ and not as graduates of a business college.

Today we talk much about the threat of atheistic Communism, and we are critical of it, as we should be. But there is curiously little said concerning Christianity's responsibility for that atheism. Why did this revolutionary movement make godlessness one of the foundations of its teaching? We can hardly escape the re-

[5] Quoted by Parsons, *Religion in Life,* Autumn, 1949.
[6] Forsyth, *The Work of Christ,* Independent Press, 1946, xix.

sponsibility of the Church. Jacques Maritain confesses our common guilt:

It is, I hold, because it originates chiefly through the fault of a Christian world unfaithful to its own principles, in a profound sense of resentment, not only against the Christian world, but—and here lies tragedy—against Christianity itself. . . .[7]

After all, when the Church no longer produces saints, what is it to produce? We may as well leave the whole business to the service clubs and the social groups. They, too, believe in respectability, but our righteousness must exceed theirs.

We cannot leave this in the midst of generalities, however, for we who have been commissioned to be leaders of the Church must feel guilt when we examine our own hearts. As a contemporary monk puts it:

Do not be too quick to condemn the man who no longer believes in God: for it is perhaps your own coldness and avarice and mediocrity and materialism and sensuality and selfishness that have killed his faith.[8]

If there is one among us who, in the wakeful hours of a troubled night, does not remember occasions when he put stumbling blocks into the path of one of Christ's children, he is an exceptional man and blessed. Most of us will have to confess that we have weakened faith and destroyed belief, and for every instance we can remember, there have been two we did not see. In the quiet moments, when we see our ministry as God must look at it, we know that these are our real failures, rather than the times the morning offering fell below expectation.

Ours is a constant ministry which goes on every hour of the day and every day of the year. The priest who tried to excuse

[7] *Man's Disorder and God's Design*, III, 96.
[8] Merton, *op. cit.*, 105.

his drunkenness by insisting that he was never drunk on duty quite misunderstood his task, and the examining bishop was right when he asked: "When is a clergyman not on duty?" It comes to us from time to time that our influential acts are often when we are not on official duty. We hear sometimes about a careless word, a small act, a hurried reply, a careless gesture which, for good or ill, carried influence. We discover also that it is the minor point in the sermon which carries the message to some soul in the congregation. No man is clever enough to guard against giving himself away somewhere in the midst of the day's work. The only safety is to be right within. Augustine's admonition to love God and do as you please goes to the center of the matter. If we can say honestly, "Lord, thou knowest all things; thou knowest that I love thee," we experience a wonderful sense of release. We shall not escape criticism, of course, but we shall no longer be concerned about it, for it will have lost its sting. The man who is too worried about pleasing men betrays his own inner insecurity, and for him the ministry must be a continual nightmare. But the good man will know peace, even in the midst of strife.

One of the men whom I admire the most found himself in a very vulnerable position. He was the head of a great university during a witch hunt, and he believed in academic freedom. Without any compromise he maintained his position and was severely attacked for it. But the turning point came when one of the most influential citizens of the state said to a group of leaders, "Can't you fellows see that we are dealing with a good man?" No one could deny it. They might disagree with him and they might think he was wrong in his policies. But none who knew him could doubt that he was a good man, and it cleared the atmosphere.

The Church puts great responsibility upon some of its ministers and places them in positions of authority. There are times when a decision has to be made which will greatly disappoint someone. The only safety for the fellowship then is to have the authority in the hands of a good man. One of the joys of my ministry has been the experience of serving under bishops who were good men. The Church can use all the talents of any man, but the Church is damaged when exceptional talents are divorced from the pure heart. It is not in our brilliance wherein lies our chief witness for our Lord, but in the humble devotion to His cause, and in love for the brethren.

Let us remember Alcibiades' testimony to Socrates' speaking, in Plato's *Symposium:*

When I listen to Pericles or any other orator of the day, I say to myself, "He is a good speaker," and that is all; but when I listen to Socrates, my soul is stirred, my eyes fill with tears, and I blush for the trivialities on which I spend my days."

It will be a sad day for any preacher when he forgets that his preaching power stems from a life "hid with Christ in God." Brilliant preaching can be little more than sounding brass without the saint's spirit to give it authority.

IV. SINGLE-MINDED DEVOTION

The art of writing fiction is not one I am qualified to discuss. But the results of the art are clear enough to any man who reads widely. One has to have the feeling that the author is speaking from his own heart and his own conviction. We must have the sense that what the characters are made to do, the writer would do. The minimum for the creation of a real novel is that the author feels what he writes. It is the same with the preacher. The average layman seems to me a most sympathetic and understanding man. He will not always agree with his preacher and he may want to tell him why, which is his right. But very seldom do we find a man who wants a mere echo of his own prejudices in the pulpit. If the preacher is utterly devoted to his task and has only the single ambition to preach the truth of the Gospel and build the Church, he does not need to fear his people. They are especially sensitive to single-minded loyalty. It is when they feel we lack that single, fanatical devotion to the cause that we get into trouble.

The authority of the preacher must always be affected profoundly by his personal life. You cannot listen with the same intentness to the man whose personal dealings have been below par. They will say of his most powerful sermon as was said on another occasion: "Your words frighten me but your life reassures me." The people will feel, and rightly, that if the Gospel is a workable way, it ought to function first in the life of its spokesman. It is a great thing when the people say to themselves that their preacher never announces a doctrine or urges an action which he does not himself incarnate.

The saint, whether in the pulpit or in the pew, is the hope of the world now as always. To meet a good man is like finding an oasis in the desert. He is the unanswerable argument to all our doubts. Remember Paul's long journey to Rome. We can imagine something of his perturbation as he moved toward the city as a prisoner. He had been on the way for many weary weeks. He had suffered shipwreck. At last they landed and were ready for the last lap of the journey on foot. Then comes this significant statement in the story:

And from thence, when the brethren heard of us, they came to meet us as far as Appii forum, and The three taverns: whom when Paul saw, he thanked God, and took courage. (Acts 28:15)

So it is with us on our journeys. Some good man comes to meet us and cheer us on our way. The hearts that have been heavy grow lighter and courage that has ebbed away flows back. The most refreshing, encouraging experience men have is to be met by someone who has heard Christ's call to be a saint.

An Episcopal bishop reported that a man who knew Russia

well had said to him, "In Russia today the only people who can be recognized as *persons* are the Christians." [9] Russia is an extreme case of a general disease which has infected our time. But there are other places, too, where it becomes increasingly difficult to recognize persons. We are the victims of terrible, mighty depersonalizing forces. Our only safety is in keeping clear in our minds that we are the sons of God, which is to say, we are persons. If the Church has lost the sense of its chief obligation to produce saints, who are the real persons, its witness will be wavering. The time has come when Christian preachers and laymen ought to re-examine the New Testament assumption, that Christians are called to be saints. It may well be that this will be God's way of destroying the dehumanizing forces which threaten this generation.

[9] Neill in *Renewal and Advance*, 77.

8

The Leader

Can the blind lead the blind? shall they not both fall into the ditch?
LUKE 6:39

THE position which the minister occupies as leader of his
church is one of the most important and yet one of the most
difficult to fill. He cannot escape it through any maneuvering.
If the church is to grow, he must give it vision and help make its
plans. If it fails to grow, he must assume the responsibility. Now
and again you find a man who disclaims either credit or blame
for what happens to the program of his church. It is in vain. If
it succeeds, he may receive more credit than he deserves, but if it
fails, he will receive more blame than he has earned. In any case,
he stands out in the open to be judged of men, as the one most
responsible.

It is possible, of course, for a man to be too much the head of
the organization. Protestantism often encourages this by referring
to churches as Dr. Blank's church. A weakness characteristic of
many a Protestant minister is an assumption that he ought to
direct and carry out the whole program of the church. A great
number of ministers do too much. They play the part of every
man from the janitor on down, and as a result they are not the
servants of the Church, but its errand boys. They never develop a
strong organization precisely because they give no one else a
chance to function. When they leave, the whole thing collapses

and the next man has to begin from the ground up. The test of a man's leadership is what happens to his church after he leaves. It is no compliment to him or to his ministry if men have not been trained to fulfill their responsibilities in the life of their church.

One of the main tasks of the minister is to create active and skilful laymen. There are a large number of churches which have been under the control of too few men for too many years. One should not minimize the service of these little groups, but even when they act from the best of motives, they are killing the Church with kindness. Every man has some service he can give to Christ through his church, and he ought to have an opportunity to give it. There are untouched sources of leadership practically everywhere. The minister's task is to ferret it out and put it to work. To this end, it would seem wise to me that every church should adopt a rotating system for electing its official members and committee personnel. It is important, however, to make each man stay off for one year after his term of service. Otherwise there is a pressure to renominate the same people. The useful man will still find ways to serve his church in other capacities and he will be called back to his service after his short leave of absence. The unprofitable servant may be encouraged to increase his efficiency or he may be quietly relegated to the ranks.

Whatever system may prove useful, it is certainly the minister's job to spread the leadership as widely as possible. At the end of any pastorate there ought to be more laymen who know the workings of the organization because of their experience as leaders. A limited participation in operating the machinery of the church weakens the fellowship. There may be a few who subscribe to the philosophy of the "indispensable man," but most Americans still believe that nothing depends on just one man, or even on one small group of men.

The minister will now and then run into the problem of the one-man church. He can make two very serious mistakes. For one thing, he may just accept the situation and go along because it is the easiest way. This will be the road chosen by the man who prefers personal comfort to building the kingdom. But a minister can make just as great a mistake by assuming an open war is inevitable from the beginning. Many a church boss can be converted, and we ought to keep our faith alive to that possibility. There are times when he can be enlisted to help spread the leadership around. But this is always a place where a man ought to give the impression that he is facing a total task, and this particular problem is not the object of his whole campaign. Very often there is a considerable group within the church which is aware of the situation and will co-operate with the minister in alleviating it. One-man churches are usually no more popular with the laymen than they are with the ministers. The minister need not assume that the working out of the problem will be his job only, for he will have much help from the members.

It is most important that the minister should have the idea he is not to lead only within the confines of the church, but he is to lead *the Church*. We are in grave danger when we become the private chaplains of our members. The field of the Church's activity is outside itself. In this, an organization can become like a man—sick with introspection. I visited a church one time and talked with several of the trustees. Not a man had a vision of the tremendous scope of the Christian opportunity in that community. They were whining about past defeats and ancient wrongs. They were living in the past and so engrossed in fitting a little program to a shrunken budget, that a church which marched like a mighty army was utterly incomprehensible to them. Men like that must not be allowed to decide policies and plan programs. A minister must find some way to by-pass them and work with men who see the Church as an instrument to be used of God to save the world. When a man gets the idea that God's chief business is saving and preserving the Church, he ought never be allowed to speak for it. It might be that the Church is no longer worth saving.

The value in John Wesley's oft-quoted word—"The world is my parish"—lies in its assumption that the Church's responsibility is as wide as the world. It is easy to withdraw into some safe place and let the world go by. It is always a temptation to lose the missionary vision and the missionary impulse. Then comes the situation described in Jesus' brief parable—the blind lead the blind and they all fall into the ditch of their mutual self-concern. To prevent this is one of the chief responsibilities of the preacher and he must have the vision of the Church's task ever before him. Then if he does his work well, Christ will perform the ancient miracle again and open blind eyes.

There is an old story about a man who rushed down the street breathlessly asking which way the crowd had gone. When someone asked him why he was so anxious to know, he replied, "I have to find them. I'm their leader." That has many applications in these days of the pollsters, but its implication for the preacher is especially clear. It is easy for a man to assume that he must always go where the majority want to go. He may ease his conscience by saying that, after all, he cannot go contrary to his people. Quite so! But the man who simply drifts with the people betrays them and his Lord. He ought to be a leader, not a blind man groping in the darkness with other blind men. He must, therefore, be ahead of the people so they feel the tug of his vision.

A man can go wrong in the other direction and take his way heedless of the people. There are men who brilliantly ride alone with very little concern as to whether their church is going their way or not. An older minister one time helped me by saying, "A locomotive running down the track alone is spectacular. It can travel fast. But a locomotive ought to pull a train. That was why it was built." We will do well to remember that when leadership moves out of sight of the people it is of little value to them.

There are men whose ministries through the years have been nothing but a desertion of their flocks. Granted they may have been right and they may have been ahead of their time. Granted they had courage and stated their beliefs fearlessly. Yet their constructive work within the fellowship was practically nil. Let such men as these find their work elsewhere. We must remember that we are the servants of the Church.

We are to be neither master nor servant of one another, but altogether, minister and people are to be the servants of Christ. The minister who has the sense of his stewardship to Someone above the Church will neither drift with the crowd nor desert the congregation. We must not claim authority where we do not deserve it nor where it is outside the realm of our service. Every great ministry has been one that knew what the goal of the Church was and has carried the people toward it through the years. We need to live so close to our Leader that we do not mistake our own ambitions for the legitimate goals of his purposes. It is a large responsibility, but the minister must never shirk it.

I. Leadership Gone Wrong

In our generation we have put much emphasis on the idea of leadership. The concept of a Führer was the central point of totalitarianism. It was the inevitable swing away from a directionless drifting and a way of life which despised discipline and called it freedom. The swing of the pendulum was extreme, and from insisting that each man had a perfect right to do as he pleased, men swung to the position which regarded one man as divinely appointed to command a nation. His slightest whim was to be obeyed and he was exalted as one divinely anointed. This was at least a release from the intolerable situation where men simply drifted. They would rather obey the dictator than be condemned to the meaningless existence of blind wandering.

The whole philosophy back of this trend assumed that salvation is from men. It was believed, and is still believed in more quarters than we care to contemplate, that a man will appear who knows all the answers and can give all the directions. To doubt him is assumed to be sin, and to disobey him is accepted as criminal. Finally the supreme crime is defined as the desire to be a person and make one's own decisions. In the totalitarian state, salvation is anonymity. It is easy to see how completely anti-Christian this idea is, for it denies belief in man and his relation to God. It is possible only on the basis of atheism or in terms of racial and national theories which are the enemies of the Christian world view.

This lust for men who will save a people is the product of faithlessness and irreligion. The cry for leadership is always loudest when men have lost their way and have no confidence in themselves. It seems to them at such times that a "strong man" is the answer, and with a kind of mass masochism they want to fall down before a ruler and bare their backs to his lash. It is one of the strange things about us that only when we see ourselves through the eyes of Jesus do we see all men in their proper perspective. When the Christian view of man is dimmed, we can be made to believe the most superstitious things about a leader.

In the age of faith, each man has a sense of his own worth and his own responsibility. He knows there is no magical answer to the problems of mankind. He will not follow the demagogue who promises profit without investment. He will make his own judgments and carry his own load. He will seek a chance to lead in the right direction. The outcry for supermen is always a sign of a sick generation. They demand a sign and a miracle, and we may judge the sincerity and worth of a candidate for leadership by his willingness or his refusal to satisfy the request.

The leadership of a people is produced by the people. Great men do not come like creatures from some heavenly planet. They come out of the life of a society and they are shaped by its faith. So it is that in the days when leaders do not seem to be especially needed, we have more than enough to supply the demand. But when we are not producing them, that is just the time we need them the most and we cry the loudest for them to appear. In those desperate times the cheap, the loud, the ruthless and the evil simplifiers have their opportunity.

In this, as in most things, we get what we deserve. The leadership of a people is always a judgment on the people and a description of their life. If we get the second-rate politician in too great percentage, that is because our political life has become second-rate. If education cannot recruit enough teachers to supply its needs, that simply means that a people has aimed its chief enthusiasm in another direction. The kind of men we recruit for the ministry is a reflection on what the Church has allowed the status of the ministry to become. People are not debauched by their leaders until they have prepared their hearts for the debauchery. No people and no organization can ever escape responsibility for its leadership. Betrayal by the leaders is one of the crucial events in a people's history, for then they either go through the fire and become purified, or they sink even deeper into their degradation. Men may postpone the inevitable debacle by surrendering their liberties, but it will be even worse because of its postponement. You cannot make gods out of men and escape the ultimate tribulation.

We shall not find it hard to see the dangerous parallels of this false leadership in the Church. We saw it in the Middle Ages and it was one of the main causes of the Reformation. There is a pride and egotism which takes hold of ministers and priests and is worse than when it appears anywhere else. For men can go to any extreme with a sinful sense of justification if they are working within a holy institution. It was an awareness of this that made Protestantism put the control of the Church back into the hands of the people. But there is nothing automatic in this arrangement, and the lust of power can control laymen as well as clergy. Whenever a man puts his way above the way of the

Church and considers himself too highly, then we see the Abomination of Desolation standing where it ought not.

There is a helpful admonition for us in the Gospel:

The disciple is not above his master: but everyone that is perfect shall be as his master" (Luke 6:40).

The sensitive preacher knows that there are saints in the congregation who are his masters in the things that count. The Church, when it is at its best, exercises a mutual criticism which keeps any single person, including the minister, from false pride. In the hour of our great dangers we can be saved if we have not withdrawn from the fellowship.

There is a temptation which comes to the brilliant preacher to think of his place as being above the Church. He comes to see himself as an end and not as a means to the building up of the people. Because he commands the largest salary in the state and preaches to the largest congregations, he will be tempted to consider his leadership as something above criticism. He may find himself assuming that it is by his might rather than by the spirit of the Lord that the kingdom prospers. He will be inviting people to come unto him and sit at his feet. A constant problem is how to keep our own egos from blocking off the road to Jesus Christ. One of our most unlovely characteristics is a tendency to stardom. Our only hope is to preach Christ and not ourselves and to keep our hearts open to the promptings of the Holy Spirit. It will help us further if we have a wife who can speak the truth to us in love.

At the Battle of the Somme, Donald Hankey led his men in a charge against the enemy. His summons is worth our remembering:

Come on, lads, come. If we get through we'll thank God; if we get wounded it's Blighty; if we go west, it's the Resurrection.[1]

[1] MacLean, *op. cit.*, 30.

That is true leadership that points clear through to God. We must be able to lead beyond tragedy and death. We have no facile answers and no extreme personal promises to make. We have our faith and the assurance of God in Christ. If we are leaders of the people, we are also followers of the Galilean and we are only taking them along with us to him.

II. MEN NEED LEADERS

The dictators show their lack of confidence in the people by despising them. The people are not regarded as capable of making any decisions and they must be ruled with an iron hand. One of the most terrible things about totalitarian systems is their complete distrust of humanity and their hatred of men. They dare not believe that men, left to themselves, will choose the road to greatness. But the democracies hold at the center of their political philosophy a belief that when the public knows what it ought to want it usually asks for it. Men can be misled and misdirected, but one of the most encouraging things to observe is how nearly always when an issue has been brought out into the open the people show taste and judgment in deciding it.

Yet men can often be mistaken concerning their desires, even when they have a clear inkling that they lack something essential. In that situation the minister must associate himself with the needs of men and dissociate himself from their unworthy desires. Men may insist that they can get what they ought to have by following an easy path, but the minister must insist that it will be obtained only by way of the Cross. When the crisis is between men who want to be saved, but not by the way of accepting Christ, then the Christian leader must forget his own personal fortunes and bear his witness manfully.

In this he has the example of his Lord, for Jesus could have identified himself with the Pharisees and their plan of national regeneration. He could have done it with clear conscience because there was much in it that was noble and right. Or he could have taken over the leadership of the functional devotion of the revolutionists and there is hardly any limit to the power he might have held. However, when he accepted the people's needs but repudiated their way of satisfying them, he went to the Cross. Yet the leadership he rejected seems to us a poor thing compared to the glory of the leadership he gained. It is sometimes necessary for us to give up an immediate influence and popularity that we may become more than passing influences in the lives of men.

Herman Melville had something of this exalted idea of the position of the pulpit:

What could be more full of meaning?—for the pulpit is ever this earth's foremost part; all the rest comes in its rear; the pulpit leads the world. From thence it is the storm of God's quick wrath is first described, and the bow must bear the earliest brunt. From thence it is the God of breezes fair or foul is first invoked for favorable winds. Yes, the world's a ship on its passage out, and not a voyage complete; and the pulpit is its prow.[2]

It may be that Melville would have been more impressed with the accuracy of his description in his time than in ours, but at least this is an accurate description of what the pulpit ought to be. The minister needs to see the rocks ahead before anyone else and give the warning in plenty of time. He ought to see the veer in the wrong direction and describe what lies ahead. Men do not suddenly lose their way and go wrong, but are put off the course by degrees when they get careless. They do not look far enough ahead, and the public will often trade freedom for security without foreseeing the disillusioning waiting if that bargain is made.

We have overdone the worship of the "common man" and we have made him the foundation of a dead-level philosophy which is ridiculous. We ought never to glorify the mediocre and the unexceptional. The concept of the "common man" has value only

[2] Melville, *Moby Dick,* Ginn & Company, 1928.

when we are speaking of what all men hold in common. The Gospel does not believe that every man is of the same stature, but only that each man is equally the object of God's love. There is a vast difference! When we are willing to elect men to high office simply because they have never taken a stand on any issue, we are entering a decadent period in our political life. It is a sad thing for us when we try to keep exceptional leaders under suspicion and make them inferior to party hacks and demagogues. This present tendency shows a total misunderstanding of our history and of our spirit.

A people will be led by someone. If they are not to be guided by churchmen, then it will be by nonchurchmen. One of the greatest mistakes we make as preachers is to assume that it is safest and best to follow the community instead of lead it. The failure of the Church in our time is often its timidity. It does not move ahead, but waits to see which way the influential citizens are going. It shrinks from announcing a proposition that will go against the prejudices of the ignorant. It adjusts its program of race relations and social justice to the yellow press. Criticism seems to be the thing which must be avoided at all costs. There is no "turning the world upside down" in it. Then while it seeks safety, it finds only emptiness and disregard. Finally it has its reward—it is ignored and passed by. Many a church becomes like a choir director I saw one time who never looked at the choir and they never looked at him. All he did was wave his stick, which, as far as could be observed, had no influence on tempo or harmony. When the Church decides to follow and not lead, it simply goes through motions which have no effect on anyone.

Much of this spirit is the fault of the minister. We have played down our special knowledge and our calling. We have leaned over backward in assuring men that we are in no way different from the average. It has seemed necessary to many of us that we should become known for our wit and conviviality, but never for our spiritual insight. I doubt that any generation of preachers has ever gone quite so far in attempting to destroy its identity as has this one. As a result, what is the most common form of approbation the average minister receives? He is happy if his laymen say, "He is a regular fellow. He preaches short sermons. He never makes you feel uncomfortable. He fits in with any crowd." None of these may be bad qualities in themselves, I agree, but when this is the sum total of the picture of a spiritual leader, it ought to make us ashamed.

It is no wonder that many laymen think their ideas of God, picked up at Sunday school forty years ago from a teacher whose theology was on a fifth grade level, are as sound as their preacher's. For he no longer stands out in their experience as a man who knows more than they do about anything. It is a strange thing that in a day of specialization the minister shrinks from being regarded as an expert even in the field of religion. We are simply preparing our people to turn to the esoteric sects for the saccharine nonsense they call religion. It would seem that, in the realm of theology at least, the minister ought to deserve and demand a place of leadership. For one of the dangerous elements in our life now is the vast amount of Christian illiteracy. Brethren, let us assume our ordination vows and become leaders of the people. The world of our generation is like the sorcerer Elymas, who was stricken with blindness and went forth "seeking some to lead him by the hand" (Acts 13:11).

Whenever the Church is under attack, then a man's leadership is tested. If hysterically he runs for cover, that proves his unworthiness for his position. Now and again you will find such a man whose only concern is for his own personal safety. If by joining in the clamor of the heresy hunters he feels there is more profit to be obtained, he will do it. Such men are beneath our contempt! But if a hysterical layman or two can stampede a congregation, that too is a judgment on the insufficiency of the minister's leadership. For the people ought to feel that, because they can trust their minister, they will wait for his word. If the Church is vital, it will be attacked and this will work out to its future benefit if preachers have the confidence of the laity. Without that confidence, a man's ministry is weighed and found wanting.

There is nothing in the teaching or example of Jesus to encourage a leaderless interpretation of the ministry. When, for example, he reproved James and John for their selfish request to sit in the favored places in his kingdom, he closes the incident with these words:

But to sit on my right hand and on my left hand is not mine to give; but it shall be given to them for whom it is prepared. (Mark 10:40)

Then he went on to contrast the basis for leadership in his movement with that among the Gentiles. The great shall be those who serve, and the chief ones shall be the servants of the others. But there is no denial of the necessity for leadership. He was concerned as to what would happen to his disciples after he was killed.

And when they had sung a hymn, they went out into the mount of Olives. And Jesus said unto them, All ye shall be offended because of me this night: for it is written, I will smite the shepherd, and the sheep shall be scattered. (Mark 14:26–27)

Our Lord never gave the impression that he was anything less than a leader. We have not fulfilled our obligations as his ministers unless we regard ourselves as appointed to be leaders of the people in his name.

Now and again there has appeared a man who fulfilled his obligations as a leader of his church and community so satisfactorily that he became a symbol of this function of the ministry. Richard Baxter was such a man. He lived his life in the village of Kidderminster which, under no circumstances, would have been chosen deliberately as the ideal setting for a historic ministry. The people were drunken and irreligious. Yet, from this place Baxter exerted an influence that went around the world and never ceased. Dean Stanley's testimony nearly two hundred years after Baxter's death is one of the highest compliments any preacher could receive:

> There have been three or four parishes in England which have been raised by their pastors to a national, almost a world-wide fame. Of these the most conspicuous is Kidderminster; for Baxter without Kidderminster would have been but half himself; and Kidderminster without Baxter would have had nothing but its carpets.[3]

It would be foolish to assume that all of us could do likewise. But all of us can accept our obligation to be more than followers of the community. We can do our part toward bringing the pulpit back to its place of authority and inspiration, which it is meant to hold. Most of our failure as leaders is our failure to see clearly the implications of our position. We betray man and God if we let ourselves be relegated to the ranks of followers of the contemporary voices. If the Church is to save the world, it has to begin to lead the world.

III. LEADERSHIP AND PRESSURE

Preaching, when it is right, answers the questions men are asking. It deals with the relevant affairs of life. It gives each man the feeling that in Christ there is the thing he seeks and the answer to his most pressing problem. Preaching that is vague and academic is quite useless because it exerts no pressure. John Wesley spoke to the poor about the riches of the Gospel and he spoke to the rich about the Gospel's demand for charity. Conversion is possible for a man when the Gospel's pressure is brought to bear on a man's particular sin.

[3] Quoted by Martin, *op. cit.*, 29.

The leadership of Jesus was this constant pressure on the sin of the group or the individual to whom he spoke. Thus he never let the Pharisees feel relaxed and at ease, in spite of their ritual and their obvious moral superiority. He found the weakness and he brought to bear all the force of his spiritual genius at that point. When he dealt with the Priests, he threw them on the defensive with his clear analysis of their pretense and pride. But they could never escape that sense of judgment, and the shame it brought to them made their selfishness a source of embarrassment.

Jesus did this with individuals. Much more than we can ever hope to attain it, he had the gift of sensing the right place to exert the pressure. Zacchaeus might never have been stabbed to his conscience if we had dealt with him. We would not have seen his hunger for honesty and our words would have been misdirected. The Rich Young Ruler would have fooled us and we would have told him he was good enough and to stop worrying. But Jesus knew the place where each man was weak and the point at which he could be urged toward a decision. There was in his presence a divine tension which became the means of conversion.

The pastor who has the sense of his opportunity will become more and more skillful in dealing with men as Jesus did. We are not to drift helplessly with the group. We are not to allow one small-visioned man to block the work of the Church. We are to exert an influence and point the way. We are to be a gentle but persistent pressure on the life of the Church and the community. We can act too fast and have too little patience. But we can also take too long and be too willing to wait for time to accomplish something. Once we have surrendered to the spirit of following the people and not leading them, we are useless in influencing spiritual growth.

It would be a good thing if every preacher should consider the year's work in terms of spiritual growth. Let us leave for the moment the increase in the budget, the improvement of the property and the increase in attendance. Let us consider the attitude of the Church toward missions, for example. Has it become more aware of its missionary responsibility and opportunity? Is there more of an inclination to accept maximum quotas rather than minimum ones? Is there less foolish talk in the board meetings about secondary matters and more statesmanlike planning? Is there less concern with silly little items which ought to be given short shrift in an important fellowship? Has the Church taken any position a step ahead of the community? Has it gone on record as favoring some Christian action in the city? Such questions as these are so seldom asked and yet they define the spiritual growth of the Church and they measure a minister's leadership.

I cannot help but feel that it is a cause for shame when a man has been in a church for any length of time and pettiness still rules its deliberations and actions. Such things are not overcome at once, but when a church has been served by a great leader, there are some things it is ashamed to do and say. Smallness is always more obvious when it is in the presence of greatness, and it is the task of the preacher to hold before his people "the habitual vision of greatness." We shall never succeed in making every man great in vision and action, but we can keep the small grumbling away from the center, and we can hold before the Church its high calling. We are not to be merely high pressure salesmen for our pet projects. But we are to be, through the grace of God, the channels of God's constant pressure on His Church.

I had conducted a funeral service on a February day in the Middle West and was on my way to the cemetery in the car leading the funeral procession. The man driving was a friend of mine and we talked together until we arrived at the cemetery entrance, where we were halted by an attendant. His first question was: "Where is the procession?" We looked back and no car was in sight. They had been blocked on an icy slope and came along about ten minutes later. But I shall never forget my consternation when we learned that the procession we thought we were leading was not there. Ministers can do their work under the same misapprehension. It is not enough for us to go our way without a backward look. We had better concern ourselves with our responsibility to keep the people with us as we move forward toward the standards of Christ.

IV. LEADER'S AUTHORITY

In a certain European country where the Church was at low ebb, the people said of their ministers: "For six days of the week our pastors are invisible! On the seventh they are incomprehensible!" [4] Laymen sometimes feel that this is an apt description of our work. They have no clear idea of what we are trying to do or say. Often this is true because we have no clear idea about these matters either.

The authority by which we lead our people has to rest ultimately in our own religious experience. This is not something that happens overnight and it does not always happen in seminary. But the purpose of the seminary is not to establish set patterns of experience. It is to plough up the mind and let the rain and sunshine of God have a chance to produce something. If young men coming from seminary are not settled in their religious beliefs and not yet established in their theology, this may be the necessary price we ought to pay for other values received.

But we can be sure that, soon or late, a man's ministry and influence will depend on his own spiritual knowledge of God. Indeed, his usefulness cannot rise higher than this ultimate source. There will come to the man who seeks, this authoritative seal of

[4] *Man's Disorder and God's Design*, I, 110.

experience. Suddenly he knows that this is the Gospel's truth for him and here is the burden of his message. It will not be just the same as any other man's, but it will be a part of Christian orthodoxy. Horace Bushnell discovered it and jumped from his bed crying, "I have found it. I have found the Gospel." This did not mean that he was not a Christian before that time, nor that he had no understanding of Christ until that moment. It meant that the Gospel had found him with its full power and he now stood on a new authority. John Wesley's heart-warming experience was that moment in his life.

It will come to each man in its own way, for the spirit bloweth as it will. But come it must, and in that high moment, a man knows he has been granted his authority as a leader of the Church. It is the time when a man can say, "I know that Jesus was right!" It is the assurance that to preach the unsearchable riches of Christ is to preach truth. The days of preparation are now over. The day of march has come.

This will bring us a single-minded devotion to our task. It takes away the personal concerns which have claimed too much of our time and attention. In the words of the old song, we say now, "Where he leads me, I will follow." The dull drabness, characteristic of too much ministerial leadership, is gone after this experience, and we exemplify the sparkle of lives which have become a constant pageant. For until our hearts are fixed on one great goal, we lack the luster of the saints. Now we know the promise of our Lord: "Thy whole body shall be full of light" (Matthew 6:22).

Bishop Quayle wrote a great word for us:

When this preacher comes to a Sunday in his journey through the week, people ask him, "Preacherman, where were you and what saw you while the workdays were sweating at their toil?" And then on this preacher we may say reverently, "He opened his mouth and taught them saying:" and there will be another though lesser Sermon on the

Mount. And the auditors sit and sob and shout under their breath, and say with their helped hearts, "Preacher, saw you and heard you that? You were well employed. Go out and listen and look another week; but be very sure to come back and tell us what you heard and saw." That will be preaching.[5]

And that will be the reward of single-minded leadership!

[5] Quoted by Martin, *op. cit.*, 63.

Index

The Slover Lectures
SOUTHWESTERN UNIVERSITY
1950